J. B. SNELL

# EARLY RAILWAYS

OCTOPUS BOOKS

# Acknowledgments

The author would like to express his gratitude to the following for their advice and assistance in the preparation of this book: L. T. C. Rolt, A. E. Durrant, P. M. Kalla-Bishop and P. B. Whitehouse.

The author and publishers wish to thank the following owners and photographers who have made available items from their collections: P. M. Alexander, figure 112; Robert C. Bishop, figure 76; T. H. Cobb, figure 130; Messrs. Coverdale and Colpitts (William H. Coverdale Collection), figures 47, 49, 62, 79, 84, 85, 108; Derek Cross, figures 93, 105; Terence Cuneo, figure 6; Donald Duke, figure 77; A. E. Durrant, figures 67, 119; Gordon Glattenberg, title-page; P. Greenslade, figure 38; F. J. G. Haut, figures 3, 4, 63-66, 126; P. V. Hodge, figures 90, 95; J. M. Jarvis, figure 123; R. H. Kindig, figure 80; Mrs H. M. le Fleming, figures 78, 110, 111, 125; Arthur L. Lloyd, figure 103; Noel Palmer (New Zealand Railways), figure 118; A. L. Papp, Jr, figure 92; Dr P. Ransome-Wallis, figure 128; P. J. T. Reed, figures 59, 106, 113; John H. Scholes, figure 6; M. C. Schrader, figure 122; W. W. Stewart, figures 109, 118; P. B. Whitehouse, figures 91, 94, 112; Messrs Wiggins, Teape and Pirie Co Ltd, figure 6; James C. Wren, figure 89.

The following illustrations are reproduced by courtesy of the following railway companies and institutions: the Alexander Turnbull Library, Wellington, New Zealand, figures 90, 95; the Association of American Railroads, figure 58; the Baltimore and Ohio Railroad Co, figures 29, 54, 69; the British Museum, figures 2, 31, 33, 34, 43, 45, 52, 75, 82, 100-2, 114; the Deutsche Bundesbahn, figures 40, 53, 127, 129; the Library of Congress, Washington, figure 73; the Missouri Pacific Lines, figure 121; the Museen der Stadt, Vienna, figure 36; the Pennsylvania Railroad Co, figure 50; Messrs Frank T. Sabin, London, figures 15, 16, 18-21, 25, 41, 42, 55, 56; the Santa Fe Railroad Co, figure 120; the Schweizerischen Bundesbahnen, figures 57, 87, 131; the Science Museum, London, figures 1, 8, 9, 10, 11, 12, 13, 14, 17, 22, 23, 24, 35, 37, 115; the Southern Pacific Co, figure 97; the Southern Railway Co (USA), figure 46; *La Vie du Rail*, Paris, figures 32, 39, 48, 61, 70-2, 86, 107.

All the items in the William H. Coverdale collection were photographed by Brenwasser (New York); figure 91 by Messrs Colourviews Ltd; figures 5, 7, 98, 104, 116, 117, 124 by the author.

*Preceding page*
One of the handful of American railways still using steam power in commercial service is the Great Western, with fifty miles of track in north-eastern Colorado; 2-8-0 no. 51, built by Baldwin in 1906, stands at the head of a freight at Loveland in November 1960

This edition first published 1972 by
OCTOPUS BOOKS LIMITED
59 Grosvenor Street, London W.1

ISBN 7064 0043 7

PRODUCED BY MANDARIN PUBLISHERS LIMITED AND PRINTED IN HONG KONG

# Contents

# The Origins of the Railway

THERE ARE TWO ELEMENTS in the definition of a railway One is the specially prepared track, designed to carry heavy loads with reduced friction; the other is the system of guidance which makes it unnecessary for vehicles to be steered. Defined in this way, railways are very much older than most people realize. One of the differences between Greeks and Romans was that, while the Romans laboured greatly to build roads all over Europe, the Greeks characteristically saw no reason why they should go to the trouble of forming flat stone surfaces ten feet wide or more when two narrow ruts carved into the rock would serve the purpose. These rutways were the ancestors of railways; they provided a smooth and relatively friction-free running surface, combined with guidance for the wheels. From remains in various places around the Mediterranean it can be seen that their engineering was also quite sophisticated. There were sidings and passing loops, and the tracks ran wherever possible along contours to preserve a level grade.

But rutways had the disadvantage that they were impossible to build except where rock lay on or near the surface of the ground. They therefore remained a local phenomenon; a convenience here and there only, and the carts and waggons which used them ran nearly as well on Roman roads or on no roads at all. Like so many of the other arts of civilization, they were forgotten during the Dark Ages. Railways as we know them began with the first stirrings of the Industrial Revolution, in the first mines, where in confined spaces underground heavy weights had to be moved over rough surfaces and prevented from hitting tunnel sides. There are illustrations in various mining textbooks from 1530 onwards showing railways or tramways of one kind or another, the earliest in Germany. Most of these had waggons with flanged wooden wheels running on wooden rails. They soon extended out of the mine tunnels and down to navigable water, as their advantages over rough mud roads were appreciated. Perhaps the largest, and certainly the most historically important, network was in the coalfields round Newcastle on Tyne, where they were introduced in 1602. By the mid-eighteenth century there were over twenty separate lines in this area.

1 A view of Newcastle-upon-Tyne from Gateshead in 1783, showing a waggon descending the Parkmoor Waggonway to the quay, the remarkably casual driver sitting on the brakelever

One of the earliest detailed descriptions we have of these waggonways dates from 1765. The track consisted of oaken timbers salvaged from dismantled ships, with rails about 7 inches high by 5 inches broad lying on cross-sleepers (ties) two or three feet apart; the gauge was anything from three to five feet. Since gradients against the load were minimized by cuttings, embankments, and bridges, one horse could draw a waggon containing $2\frac{1}{4}$ tons of coal, compared with the four-fifths of a ton which was the most it could move on an ordinary road. On the steeper descents, which were anything up to 1 in 20 or 1 in 15 (5% to 7%), the horse was detached and the waggon ran down by gravity, the driver applying a crude brake to one pair of wheels by sitting on a lever. The view of Newcastle and the Parkmoor Waggonway in 1783 [figure 1] illustrates this process, with the waggon on the lip of a frightening declivity, the driver showing no signs of alarm, and the dejected-looking horse trailing along behind. These gradients could, however, be dangerous. The wooden rails became extremely slippery when wet and the wooden wheels lost all their adhesion. Boys were employed at the steeper places in bad weather to scatter sand and ashes on the rails, but an ill-timed shower could cause havoc and there are records of several incidents when every waggon on the line slithered uncontrollably down into a heap of ruins at the bottom of the hill.

But with wooden rails there was no prospect of any other technical improvement. Wooden wheels wore out rapidly, but the cast-iron wheels which came into use after about 1760 chewed up the rails even faster. First, renewable wooden strips were laid on top of them, and then iron straps,

2 The 'drops' at Wallsend in the early nineteenth century, where coal was transferred from rail to water; the weight of the loaded wagon caused the arm and platform to descend, and counterweights pulled the empty wagons back

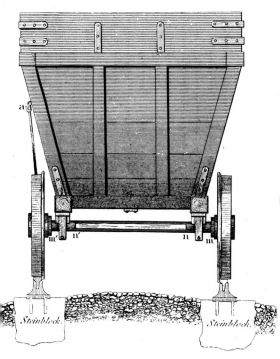

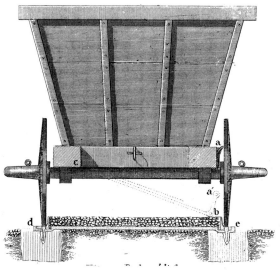

3 and 4 Two German drawings of the 1820s showing the difference between the standard edge-rail and flanged wheel system (top) and the plate-rail and plain wheel (bottom), as applied to horse-drawn wagons

but they soon worked loose. Rails made wholly of iron were needed, and it is believed that they were first made successfully by Richard Reynolds at Coalbrookdale in Shropshire in November 1767. Business at the ironworks was slack, and to avoid putting out the furnace he began to cast rails for his own waggonway, intending to take them up again when demand recovered. But they were too valuable; not only did they reduce repair costs, but a horse's payload was more than doubled by the reduced friction.

So far railways had been inseparable from mining. But the second half of the eighteenth century was the great age of canal-building, when it seemed as if inland navigation was the final solution to the transport problem. Yet canals had disadvantages which were to prove fatal. They were expensive and slow to build, and clumsy when they came to high ground; the further they rose above sea level, the worse the difficulties became, and they soon reached places where money could drive them no further. To serve localities beyond, engineers began to build feeder railways. So the new canal companies found themselves operating both forms of transport, and after a while were able to compare the results. At first railways were only used very reluctantly and on a small scale, yet as their practical advantages were demonstrated, the balance began to alter. Not long before he died in 1803, the first great British canalbuilder, the Duke of Bridgewater, remarked sourly, 'I see mischief in these damned tramroads'. Writing in 1831, Nicholas Wood quoted the case of the tramway from Brynmawr down to the Brecon canal near Govilon in South Wales, which had taken months instead of years to build. Although a mere tributary to the canal, it paid a comfortable five per cent, while the canal company with its larger traffic had not yet bettered a half per cent dividend.

One result of the canal connection was that for the first time railways began to be considered worthy of the attention of professional engineers. Some of them were not prepared to accept that the time-honoured design of flanged wheel on flangeless rail, devised by rude mechanics, was the right one, and in 1797 Benjamin Outram adopted a system which put the flange onto an L-shaped cast-iron 'plate' rail. These plateways flourished for a time, especially in South Wales, but even though their waggons could also run on roads they had several serious drawbacks. The 'plate' rail was structurally unsound; the weight of metal in the flange added little to its strength, and breakages were frequent. It also tended to collect dirt and gravel which greatly increased friction. So one by one the plateways were converted to ordinary 'edge' railways. A lone survivor lingered on in the Forest of Dean until the 1930s, but they are now extinct.

These drawbacks caused one man to reinvent the flanged wheel in 1801. For Lord Penrhyn's railway from Port Penrhyn to the Penrhyn slate quarries in North Wales, a local sage, Benjamin Wyatt of Bangor, devised an oval rail and wheels with a concave groove. This worked well enough, but the wheels wore very quickly on the narrow bearing. So Wyatt replaced the oval rail with a flat-topped one, filled in the wheel groove, and found himself with a double flange [figure 5]. This system still survives, and is in fact standard in many local quarries. Although it made for a certain amount of complication at points and crossings [figure 7], it had one advantage; since all wheels were loose on their axles, the gauge of the track did not have to be exact, and it could be laid very roughly without causing derailments.

But although some enthusiasts had visions of a nationwide system of horse tramways, they remained of local interest only. It was the introduction of steam power that transformed the railway into a force that reshaped the world.

Stationary steam engines had been used, mainly to pump water out of mines, since the beginning of the eighteenth century, but all were large and cumbersome. They used steam at very low pressure, often merely to displace air and create suction through condensation, and with their enormous cylinders and condensers they were quite unportable. To build a moving engine it was necessary to use 'strong steam', at high pressure, with smaller parts. But James Watt, who had greatly improved steam engines already, and had protected his position by a barricade of patents, considered perfection had been attained and for

5 A recent photograph of double-flanged wagon wheels on the Nantlle Railway in North Wales

6 Terence Cuneo's spirited reconstruction of the opening day of the Stockton and Darlington Railway, 27 September 1825: *Locomotion* driven by George Stephenson himself, races a coach on the section near Eaglescliffe where railway and turnpike road ran parallel

some time prevented further progress in England. It was therefore the Frenchman, Nicolas Cugnot, who in 1769 built the first self-propelled vehicle, a nose-heavy three-wheeler which ran (briefly) on the public road. In 1784 Watt's pupil William Murdoch built a model experimental steam locomotive, to the anger of his master and the distress of the Vicar of Redruth, who fled before it along the highway howling that the Devil was after him.

But Watt could not monopolize steam power indefinitely, and several other engineers made progress towards designing a workable road locomotive in England and abroad. Much

the most important was Richard Trevithick, who built one at Coalbrookdale in 1802. Samuel Homfray, a South Wales ironmaster, saw and was impressed by this machine, and invited Trevithick to build one for use on the new Penydarran railway which served his ironworks at Dowlais. This was a plateway of 4' 2" gauge, nine miles long, and Trevithick's locomotive, the first to run on rails, made a successful journey over it with a loaded train on February 13th, 1804. Successful, that is, as far as the engine was concerned; it was too heavy for the track and broke quite a number of the cast-iron tramplates, so that after its maiden voyage it was shorn of its wheels and converted into a stationary engine. But the practicability of the idea was proved, and Homfray won a wager with a friend who had said that the thing was impossible.

In this first locomotive, Trevithick had broken away from Watt's practice by using relatively high pressure (25 lbs per square inch) and by allowing the steam to expand in the cylinder before exhausting into the open air. He had thereby greatly improved the power-to-weight ratio, but as can be seen from the drawing of a locomotive which he built in 1805 for a colliery at Gateshead [figure 8] it was still a very primitive machine. There was only one cylinder, situated inaccessibly in the boiler barrel, and driving an enormous flywheel by means of a trombone-slide arrangement and two flailing connecting rods, one on either side. The boiler was advanced for its time, with a large U-shaped

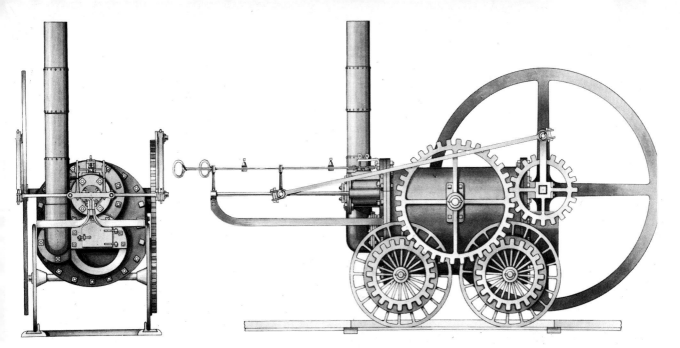

8 Richard Trevithick's second railway locomotive, built at Gateshead in 1805 and
similar to his first, which had hauled the
world's first steam train at Penydarran the
year before

return flue containing the fire at one end and the base of the
chimney at the other. The drive from the flywheel was by
means of gears. Trevithick had also seized on two important
technical points which his successors took some time to
appreciate. He knew that the ordinary friction between
smooth iron surfaces would give sufficient grip to his driving
wheels, whatever scientists might say to the contrary. He
also knew that an artificial draught was needed before the
fire would burn fiercely enough to generate sufficient steam,
and that the simplest way of producing this was to blast the
exhaust steam up the chimney.

The main reason why Trevithick's locomotives were not a
practical success was because they were too heavy for the
track. This explains why, apart from a circular demonstration line in London in 1808, he made no further progress
with the idea. Any saving in running cost which locomotives
achieved would be more than outweighed by the expense of
relaying and strengthening the railways to carry them. But
one effect of the Napoleonic Wars was to raise the price of
fodder, and the rising cost of horse haulage forced railwaymen to look at Trevithick's ideas again. John Blenkinsop,
agent of the Middleton collieries near Leeds, decided to try
out an improved system. He considered that the problem of
rail breakage could be overcome by limiting the weight of
the locomotive as far as possible, while the resulting loss of
adhesion could be compensated by a rack and pinion drive.
In 1811 he gave instructions to Matthew Murray, the

11

9 A freight train on the Liverpool and Manchester Railway, worked by a *Planet*-type 2-2-0, passing under the skew bridge near Rainhill shortly after the railway was opened

proprietor of a nearby foundry, to build two locomotives to his patent specification (with licence from Trevithick) and he ordered the relaying of the Middleton Railway with strengthened cast-iron rails which incorporated teeth on their outside edge.

Blenkinsop's engines [figure 12] were an important step forward, and completely successful. The major novelty was the use of two cylinders instead of one, thus avoiding the need for a flywheel (and for a crowbar to start the engine if it happened to stop on a dead centre). By placing the cylinders vertically in the boiler, the fireman was spared the peril of being caught up and shaken to death by the sweeping crosshead. The rack drive was well thought out, even if it was soon proved unnecessary. The curious feature of Blenkinsop's engines was that he had abandoned Trevithick's draughting; steam from the cylinders was exhausted separately, at first through a short vertical pipe, later more silently through a second chimney. Perhaps on a 3½-mile private railway like the Middleton frequent involuntary stops to raise steam pressure may not have mattered, but nevertheless this alteration seems strange. However, a train of 100 tons was hauled quite satisfactorily at 3½ mph, and the *Prince Regent* and *Salamanca* began regular work at Middleton on August 12th, 1812. They were joined a year or so later by two more, and these four locomotives worked the railway for over thirty years.

Two other British engineers were also experimenting, with less success. In 1812 William Chapman tried out an engine at Heaton Colliery which dragged itself along on a chain; there was so much friction that this feat, without a load, was all that it could achieve. In 1813 William Brunton

10 The *Northumbrian* engine, built for the Liverpool and Manchester in 1830, and the final development of the *Rocket* type

11 George Stephenson's seal

12 One of John Blenkinsop's rack locomotives which started work on the Middleton Railway near Leeds in 1812, the first to be a commercial success (the artist has omitted the tender)

patented a locomotive which pushed itself along on two grasshopper-like legs; it worked, although only in one direction, and not in any case for long, as it soon exploded and therefore owes its main claim to fame as the cause of the first serious railway accident.

William Hedley, of the Wylam colliery, a few miles west of Newcastle, was the next man to build a locomotive. The Wylam Railway, a wooden line of great antiquity, had just been rebuilt as a five-foot gauge plateway, and for it in 1813 Hedley built his famous *Puffing Billy*. Unlike Blenkinsop, who used a very inefficient boiler with a single straight flue, Hedley reintroduced Trevithick's return flue and steam blast, and also reverted to simple adhesion drive. He placed the cylinders outside the boiler, where they were more accessible. At first his engine was four-wheeled, but in this form the axle-loading was too much for the cast-iron plate rails; so, adopting an idea of Chapman, he rebuilt it on two bogies, with all eight wheels driven by gears [figure 13]. Although there must have been a terrible grinding and gnashing of teeth as it moved along, Hedley's engine was a complete success and several more were placed in service. Around 1830 the Wylam line was rebuilt as a five-foot gauge railway and the engines became four-wheelers again, in which form they continued to run until 1862. The photograph [figure 14] was taken at this time. Hedley's contribution to locomotive development is often underestimated, as he had the misfortune to be overshadowed by a greater man still.

George Stephenson was born in 1781, in a house which still stands beside the Wylam railway. By 1813 he had won a reputation as a self-taught engineer with a natural genius for machinery, but he had never tried his hand at locomotives. In that year he was appointed engineer of the Killingworth Railway, and was instructed to design and build one. His

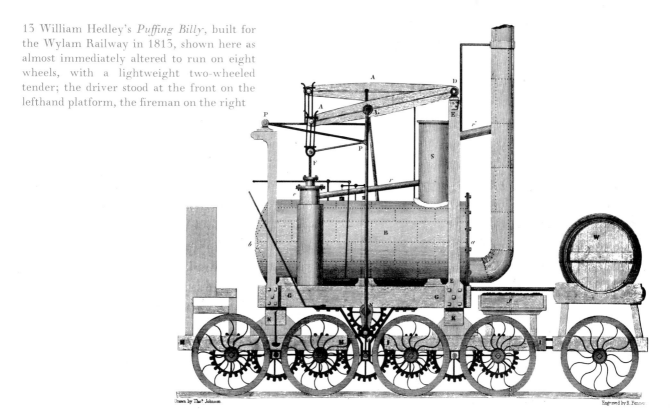

13 William Hedley's *Puffing Billy*, built for the Wylam Railway in 1813, shown here as almost immediately altered to run on eight wheels, with a lightweight two-wheeled tender; the driver stood at the front on the lefthand platform, the fireman on the right

Drawn by Thos Johnson

Engraved by R. Fenner

14 One of the *Puffing Billy* engines photographed in 1862, when the Wylam Railway was converted from five-foot to 4' 8½" gauge, and they were finally taken out of service

first, the *Blucher*, was tested in July 1814. In one respect it was unique, as no engine had ever before worked on an edge railway without a rack-and-pinion; but in every other respect it was a very conservative effort compared with Hedley's, being more or less a direct copy of the Middleton machines. However, it worked well, and Stephenson's later engines were successively improved, although he never

15 (*top*) First class passengers on the Liverpool and Manchester in 1830, and the mails, travelled comfortably in carriage with stage-coach type bodies (each individually named in the stage-coach tradition), drawn by a *Planet* class engine

16 (*bottom*) The Liverpool and Manchester's second class passengers are carried in anonymous boxes, hauled by an engine of the already obsolescent *Rocket* class

departed from the inadequate single-flue boiler and they all suffered from poor steaming and heavy coal consumption, a minor disadvantage so long as small coal was of so little value that it was used to ballast the tracks. Stephenson's two original contributions were to replace gears by coupling and connecting rods, and his steam springs. Earlier engines had all been completely unsprung, which was the cause of many broken rails, and until adequate steel springs were developed in the late 1820s, Stephenson's method of carrying the weight on a piston forced by steam to one end of a cylinder was a satisfactory makeshift.

By this time railways here and there had begun to haul freight for the public as well as for their owners, and in a few places passengers were already being carried; the Swansea and Mumbles railway in South Wales, the first to offer a regular service, entered this business in 1807. But so far no locomotive had yet been used on a public rail-

way. There was one main reason for this: people were frightened of them. Especially where some of the Tyneside lines ran through village streets, the distressing experience of the Vicar of Redruth was all too often repeated. A Scotsman travelling south on one occasion interrupted his journey near Killingworth by leaping over a hedge, shouting that he had just seen a 'terrible deevil' in the High Street. Horses were equally alarmed by the puffing, grinding and banging; fires were started by the showers of red-hot coals cascading from the chimney, and thick black clouds of smoke caused further complaints. All these evils were being mitigated, but it was a slow business. Meanwhile many people looked on locomotives as a nuisance committed by rich and powerful men in pursuit of further profit. While they ran on private railways, there was no way of preventing their use, but before they could be used on public lines, legal authority was needed, and could well be denied.

George Stephenson was appointed Engineer of the Stockton and Darlington Railway in 1821, before construction started. He brought south with him his eighteen-year-old son Robert, and lost no time in altering the original plans drawn up by his predecessor George Overton. He scrapped the specification for a plateway, and determined on an edge railway of 4′ 8″ gauge, the same as the Killingworth line (the additional half-inch was added some years later to reduce friction). Already at the back of his mind was the idea that one day railways would join into a national system, and should therefore be uniform. Finally, he persuaded the company to plan for locomotives. At the western end of the line, in hilly country, haulage was to be by fixed engines on the Brusselton and Etherley inclines, and horses elsewhere, but on the slowly descending twenty miles from Shildon to Stockton Quay locomotives were to run. It was on this section, on September 27th, 1825, that Stephenson's *Locomotion* hauled the first steam train on any public railway in the world.

It was certainly a memorable occasion. From Shildon, the train consisted of twenty-one waggons fitted with temporary seats, the solitary passenger coach *Experiment*, and ten loaded coal trucks which had come down the inclines from the Witton Park colliery early that morning. Nobody knows how many passengers there were; the company had issued three hundred tickets to shareholders, but the party was swollen by uninvited guests and there were perhaps twice this number on board. Ahead of the engine rode a man on horseback bearing a red flag. Apart from the removal of a defective wagon and an unscheduled stop to make adjustments to the feedpump, all went well. A crowd of twelve thousand watched the train pause outside Darlington; then, on the way to Stockton, where the line ran beside the turnpike

17 Built for Canadian service, and seen here at New Glasgow, Nova Scotia in 1883, the *Samson* of 1838 was the final development of Timothy Hackworth's type of locomotive

road, there was a wild scene as the train was followed by a crowd of riders, carts and carriages [figure 6]. Finally *Locomotion* rolled onto Stockton Quay to a 21-gun salute before a crowd of forty thousand.

But this was just a celebration. As the railway settled down to earn a living, locomotives had to prove themselves a better economic prospect than the horses which worked beside them, and this took some time. At first the engines were used only for coal traffic, and Timothy Hackworth, the world's first Locomotive Superintendent, who had been Hedley's assistant at Wylam, often had considerable difficulty in keeping them going. Troubles were many, and until Hackworth and Robert Stephenson replaced the original solid cast-iron wheels by stronger ones with separate wrought-iron tyres, and solved the spring problem, the cost of replacing broken wheels and rails threatened to ruin the venture. Boiler explosions also caused alarm: *Locomotion* herself, and another engine, blew up in 1828. Yet improvements were continually made through experience. As early as 1828 Hackworth was building engines with six wheels coupled, and although he never abandoned vertical cylinders, he did abandon Stephenson's original straight-flue boiler in favour of Trevithick's superior return-flue, which he later further improved. In their final form his engines lasted well and gave good service [figure 17].

All this activity in Britain was watched with keen interest in other countries, where horse-worked railways also existed. None paid closer attention than the Americans. John Stevens, who had been agitating in favour of a programme of railway construction, built a small experimental engine and demonstrated it on a circular line near New York in 1824. Stevens' engine was quite original, having a vertical watertube boiler capable of working at the astonishingly high pressure of 500 lbs per square inch (previously 'high pressure' had meant Trevithick's 25 lbs.), and a single cylinder driving through gears onto a central rack rail. However, it was no more than a toy. The first serious locomotives in America were built for the Delaware and Hudson Canal Co., which opened a sixteen-mile line from the wharf at Honesdale, Pennsylvania, to the Carbondale mines in 1829. In the previous year the company had commissioned Horatio Allen to visit England, find out what he could about locomotives, and buy some. He ordered two, one of ordinary late Stephenson type, built by Foster, Rastrick & Co. of Stourbridge, [figure 23], and a much more advanced machine from

18, 19, 20, 21 Drivers and Guards of 1832 and 1852: the artist contrasts the elegance of the coaching era with the scruffiness of the age of steam; a nostalgic viewpoint, finding its echo in Dickens, had already begun to appear.

Robert Stephenson & Co., the *America* [figure 22].

However, only the *Stourbridge Lion* ever ran. She was tried at Honesdale on August 9th, 1829, with Horatio Allen at the throttle. 'I took my position on the platform of the locomotive alone', he wrote fifty years later, 'and with my hand on the throttle-valve said "If there is any danger in this ride it is not necessary that the life and limb of more than one be subjected to that danger."' (It was not the hissing monster that was viewed with such alarm; it was a perilous bridge and curve.) 'The locomotive, having no train behind it, answered at once to the movement of the hand; soon the straight line was run over, and the curve reached and passed before there was time to think . . . Soon I was out of sight in the three miles ride alone in the woods of Pennsylvania. I had never run a locomotive or any other engine before; I have never run one since.' But although the *Stourbridge Lion* returned safely to base, she had inflicted such damage on the weak track that the idea of using steam at Honesdale was abandoned. Both engines were taken off the road and used to drive machinery.

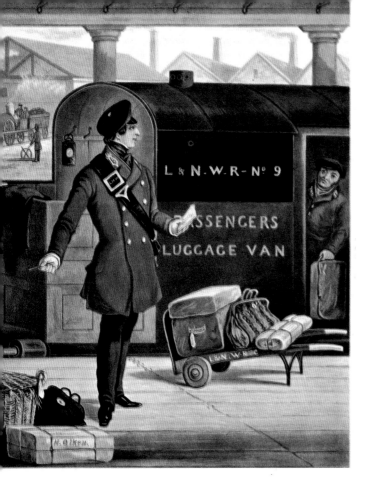 

More important in American railway history was the Baltimore and Ohio. Canal-building was then also at its height in the United States, and the city of Baltimore, because it was cut off from its hinterland by a range of hills through which there was no possibility of building a canal, feared for its future. The only answer was to build a railway. But even though its promoters had this limited object, there was no shortage of men with the wider vision of a national system of railways, and the aged Charles Carroll of Carrollton, last survivor of those who signed the Declaration of Independence, was one of them. In his speech when he laid the railway's first foundation stone at Baltimore he declared that he considered this one of the most important acts of his life, and perhaps not second even to signing the Declaration.

As soon as a few miles of track had been laid in 1829, Peter Cooper of New York demonstrated a locomotive to persuade the directors that they should use steam power. His *Tom Thumb* [figure 29] was as tiny as its name implies, hardly weighing more than a ton and developing just over one horsepower from a small vertical boiler and single

21

22 Robert Stephenson's *America*, the even less fortunate stable companion of the *Stourbridge Lion*, which never saw service in America at all (mechanically she is interesting as a halfway stage in the development from *Locomotion* to the *Rocket*)

cylinder. Yet it caused a gratifying sensation. On a famous occasion in 1830 it set off on the double track beside a horse, both pulling similar loads, and until its belt-driven blower fan broke down, it was having much the better of the race.

Another very early locomotive engineer was the Frenchman, Marc Seguin, who visited the Stockton and Darlington shortly after it opened, and in 1829 delivered two locomotives to the Lyons and St Etienne Railway, a 38-mile line of which the first section had been opened the year before. Like the Stockton and Darlington, it at first used horses as well as locomotives, although for two-thirds of its length it was sufficiently steeply inclined to allow trains to run down by gravity. Seguin's engine [figure 24] was a machine of remarkable originality. Although he still used vertical cylinders, he mounted them and arranged the drive in such a way that a certain amount of springing could be given to the wheels. Like Peter Cooper, Seguin evidently mistrusted the steam blast, and the most conspicuous feature was the pair of rotary blowers mounted on the tender. These were driven by a belt from one of the tender wheels, and blew the fire through two flexible leather pipes. Of course, this arrangement was no improvement, especially on a line with a constant gradient, as the fire would be blown much more fiercely when the engine was coasting freely downhill than when it was climbing slowly. As can be seen from the print showing complete trains [figure 32], Seguin soon discarded these blowers and reverted to the steam blast.

23 The *Stourbridge Lion*, the first main-line locomotive to operate in the United States; it was not highly regarded by its owners at the time, but this painting by A. Sheldon Pennoyer was commissioned by the Delaware and Hudson Company 100 years later

More original was Seguin's boiler, which was an interesting half-way measure between Trevithick's return-flue arrangement and the multi-tubular modern type with which Robert Stephenson was even then experimenting on the *Rocket*. Seguin placed the fire under the boiler barrel, surrounded by a water-jacket, with a large single flue towards the front of the boiler. But from here the hot gases returned through a large number of small tubes through the boiler barrel to the chimney above the firedoor. Seguin therefore realized, with Robert Stephenson, that many small tubes with a larger total surface area heated the water more effectively than one big tube of equal cross-section; and that by this means the fire could be made smaller, the rain of sparks from the chimney lessened, and efficiency increased.

By 1829, therefore, steam locomotives were operating in England and France and had been demonstrated in America. But so far no railway depended on them absolutely; they were still only an alternative to horses. It was the Liverpool and Manchester which became the world's first modern railway, linking two cities and wholly worked by mechanical power. The construction of this line was George Stephenson's most important achievement, but to succeed he and his supporters had first to win three crucial battles.

To start with, they had to win the power to build at all, and the fight before Parliament was long and ferocious. Against the railway were many powerful interests. The canal proprietors, ignoring complaints that freight often took longer to reach Manchester from Liverpool than Liverpool from New York, feared the loss of their monopoly, and so did the stage coach owners. A solid phalanx of landowners offered total obstruction. Some of these no doubt opposed the scheme because they believed the rumours put about by those with vested interests, that smoke from the engines would choke men, kill birds and cause cows to run dry; others certainly opposed it in the confident, happy and well-justified expectation that they would be richly bribed to desist. In later years many landowners mastered this technique to a nicety; their opposition was fierce enough to ensure a generous settlement, but not usually so fierce as to risk any actual deviation of the line. The sincere and uncompromising foe was rare, but rarer still was the landowner who in one case refunded his compensation to the railway, saying that ten years' experience had proved that his estates 'had not suffered to the degree anticipated'. The opposition was never fiercer than on the Liverpool and Manchester, where Stephenson's surveyors were set upon by hired gangs of toughs, hunted by gamekeepers and so chivvied that they often had to work by night, while eagle-eyed lawyers in Parliament scrutinized their plans for any resulting inaccuracies.

Stephenson's second battle came with the actual construction of the line. It was one of the biggest civil engineering works yet undertaken, and quite new techniques were needed to solve some of the problems, notably the crossing of Chat Moss, then a treacherous bog on which no man could walk.

24 A model of Marc Seguin's locomotive built for the Lyons and St Etienne Railway in 1829 – two plates have been removed from the top of the boiler to show the tubes inside, and the two belt-driven blowers are conspicuous

25 The London and Birmingham under construction: blasting rocks just north of the Linslade tunnel in October 1837

But his third battle was fought mainly in private on the question of haulage. At this time, using either horses or relatively feeble locomotives, it was considered the soundest practice to grade a railway rather as if it were a canal: to run as far as possible on the level or on a very easy gradient, and to concentrate all changes of height into short steep lengths, like flights of locks. These inclines lent themselves to working by ropes and stationary engines, since power could be economised with the descending train balancing the ascending once. It was now proposed to use this system to work the level sections also, and several distinguished engineers supported the idea. In the event it was never used on a large scale, as the practical difficulties were seen to be too great; 25

26, 27 and 28 The Rainhill constestants: Braithwaite's and Ericsson's *Novelty* (top), Timothy Hackworth's *Sans Pareil* (middle) and Robert Stephenson's *Rocket* (bottom)

29 (*right*) A rather larger than life-sized replica of Peter Cooper's *Tom Thumb*, the original of which was demonstrated on the Baltimore and Ohio in 1829

but the scheme was pressed on the Liverpool and Manchester Board, who finally agreed to decide the issue by a contest.

The famous Rainhill Trials were held on a 1½-mile stretch of level track which had been completed by October 1829. The company had offered a prize of £500 for a locomotive 'which should be a decided improvement on those now in use as respects the consumption of coke, increased speed, adequate power, and moderate weight'. It should be carried on either four or six wheels, should weigh no more than 4½ or 6 tons, and should be capable of hauling a load of up to twenty tons in proportion to its weight at ten miles an hour. The very severe weight limit (*Locomotion* had scaled eight tons) barred any useful engines then running. There was a flood of paper entries, perpetual motion machines and extravagant flights of disordered imaginations, for the terms of the contest had taken the public's eye; but in the event there were only three actual challengers. Braithwaite and Ericsson, an Englishman and a Swede who had been working together in London on the development of steam road carriages, entered the *Novelty*, a light four-wheeler built on road car principles. It was fast enough, comfortably exceeding thirty miles an hour with a light load. But George Stephenson remarked as she flashed past to the crowd's cheers, 'We've no need to fear yon thing; she's got no guts', and he was right. Successive breakdowns put her out of the running.

The second entry was Timothy Hackworth's *Sans Pareil*,

PETER COOPER'S "TOM THUMB" 1829-30 BALTIMORE & OHIO R.R.

30 One of the Baltimore and Ohio's *Grasshoppers* in its final form in the early nineties (the small four-wheeled tender is not shown)

31 St Hilda's Pit, Wallsend, in the 1820s – an early railhead in the Northumbrian coalfields, with winding and pumping enginehouses, pithead buildings and wagons under repair

a reduced four-wheeled version of his standard Stockton and Darlington engine. But she was overweight, extravagant in fuel, and unlucky. The boiler sprang a leak at a critical moment, and when oatmeal was put into the water to staunch it, as was then standard practice, the feed pump became blocked with porridge.

The only engine to fulfil the terms of the competition was Robert Stephenson's *Rocket*. On his return in 1827 from three years in South America, he had devoted himself to improving locomotive design, which had changed little in a decade or more. He had already introduced springs and abandoned the old vertical cylinders by the time he built the ill-fated *America*, but with the *Rocket* he introduced the fundamental improvement of the multi-tube boiler, and her resulting superior steam-raising and fuel economy at Rainhill clinched her victory. For the last of the stipulated loaded journeys the *Rocket*, which had hitherto been restrained to an average of only 14 mph, was given her head and reached 29 mph, almost the *Novelty's* maximum, with a full load. Having proved their point and won the prize, the Stephensons demolished the claims of the stationary engine by hauling coachloads of passengers unofficially up the 1 in 96 (1 %) Sutton Incline, which had always been intended for cable haulage, at 20 mph.

Eighteen months later the Baltimore and Ohio also held a locomotive competition. The weight limit was even stricter than at Rainhill; no engine was to exceed $3\frac{1}{2}$ tons. But the

32 Trains on the Lyons and St Etienne in the early 1830s: horse-drawn first and second class carriages, horse-drawn goods wagons, carriages coasting down from St Etienne to Givors, and coaltrucks drawn by a locomotive

other conditions of the contest, that each engine should satisfactorily complete thirty days in general service, hauling fifteen tons at fifteen miles an hour, were more realistic and the prize money ($4000 first, $3500 second) considerably more generous. As a further act of goodwill, the company agreed to provide tenders for all engines entered. There were five competitors, and the winner was the watchmaker Phineas Davis, whose vertical-boilered *York* became the prototype of the Baltimore and Ohio's first fleet of locomotives. These eighteen 'grasshoppers' gave excellent service; the last one was not withdrawn till 1893 [figure  ]. By then they were the oldest active locomotives in the world by a considerable margin. By 1835, when the line had reached Harpers Ferry, 76 miles from Baltimore, steam was in entire command of the Baltimore and Ohio.

The Liverpool and Manchester had been officially opened

on September 15th, 1830 and the day had started as an occasion of immense splendour and dignity. But halfway along the route, where the special trains had stopped for water, William Huskisson, MP for Liverpool, ex-President of the Board of Trade, and a dogged supporter of the railway, was run over by the *Rocket* and fatally injured. The shattering effect of this disaster was balanced by the fact that the dying man had been whirled away to a doctor at 36 mph.

Although the opening was marred by other fiascos (the trains were met at Manchester by a crowd whose intentions towards the Duke of Wellington, the guest of honour, were far from friendly), the railway soon proved a triumphant success. Not only was the feasibility of steam power finally demonstrated; it was also shown to be a potential gold-mine. Having taken the previous road and canal traffic as a guide to its probable business, the company expected to make most of its money from freight, and succeeded in doing so eventually. But the number of passengers travelling between the two cities multiplied rapidly. It was now possible to live in one city and conduct business in the other, and for the first time men realized that greater speed and comfort were themselves enough to increase the number of travellers, a lesson which transport undertakings even now sometimes find hard to learn. It was appreciated soon enough in 1830, and as Liverpool and Manchester shares rose in value and the line was seen to be a great public benefit, railway projects were pressed forward with new vigour in England and abroad.

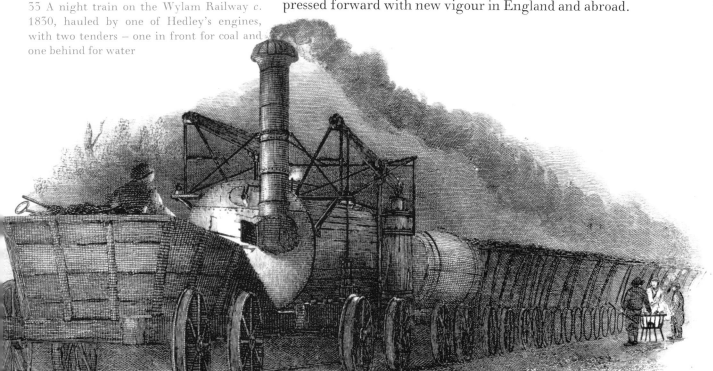

33 A night train on the Wylam Railway *c.* 1830, hauled by one of Hedley's engines, with two tenders – one in front for coal and one behind for water

# The First Main Lines (1830~70)

'NOT ONLY HAS THE QUESTION been decided, and in the most conclusive and practical manner, that railways are fitted for the conveyance of general merchandize; but with the assistance of locomotive engines, it has been proved that they are capable of effecting a rapidity of transit greater than that by any other practical mode of travelling. The greatest exertions have hitherto been used to accelerate the speed of the mails (which have hitherto been the quickest species of conveyance) without being able to exceed 10 miles an hour, and that only with the exercise of such destruction of animal power, as no one can contemplate except with feelings of the most painful nature. Upon the Liverpool Railway an average rate of 15 miles is kept up with the greatest ease, and on an extraordinary occasion, nearly double that rate, or 30 miles in one hour.'

So wrote Nicholas Wood in 1831, at a time when coach-owners expected to lose one horse every 200 miles in post-chaise work, due either to heart failure or broken legs; ordinary stage-coaches were only somewhat less murderous. Wood found ready listeners in other countries too, and the vision of national railway networks began to be generally accepted, but with differences.

In Britain there was no general plan; the development of railways was left entirely to private enterprise. It was open to anybody who considered that some particular line would be profitable to float a company and seek power and money to build it. The State simply acted as a referee. It soon established a few rules, mainly on technical points like the layout of level crossings, and for a few vital years (until it withdrew the instruction in 1836) it insisted that all railways should be built to the Stephenson standard gauge of 4′ 8½″. Where two competing projects came forward simultaneously, the State would decide in favour of one or the other. But this was as far as any actual planning of railways went. The existence of one line between two points was no bar to the construction of another, indeed to some extent competition of this kind was encouraged in order to prevent one company from gaining a monopoly. But while it did little to hinder, Parliament did equally little to help. The Liverpool and Manchester received a government loan, but it was exceptional; the task was left elsewhere to private capital. For a

34 A top-hatted policeman gives the 'all clear' to one of Gooch's *Firefly* class as it leaves a short tunnel between Bath and Bristol on the Great Western

while all went well; responsible bankers and financiers examined each scheme on its merits, and entrepreneurs were at first slow to realize how profitable railways could be. But when they did, things soon got out of hand. Any harebrained scheme would attract a hungry crowd of speculators; shoddier and shadier prospectuses multiplied, all attracting generous contributions. Some, luckier or less honest than others, made fortunes overnight and basked in temporary glory. A number of railways were actually built, although only a fraction of those put forward. In 1845-6, during the 'Railway Mania', the investing public became quite light-headed; widows and orphans rushed like sheep to buy railway shares, and were duly shorn. In reaction, raising funds for new lines became unreasonably difficult for some time afterward. Writing shortly before the Mania, a contributor to the *Athenaeum* pointed out that the concentration on building railways where they would be most profitable had harmed the national interest; parallel lines existed in some places, when the money could have been better employed in constructing trunk routes from London to Scotland, Holyhead or Plymouth. The mania may have been painful, but it cured this particular short-sightedness and all these lines were built within the next ten years.

In America railway promotion was on a similar basis; anybody proving a case for any railway could go ahead and build it. But there was one important difference. Private capital was not sufficient in many cases and government help was often needed. Sometimes, for example in Pennsylvania, the

35 Two of Edward Bury's undersized locomotives for the London and Birmingham at the entrance to the Camden Town depot

36 A spirited watercolour by Leander Russ, showing a train on the Südbahn stretch between Perchtoldsdorf and Mödling in Austria in 1847 (note the very early bogie coaches and the 'highball' signal in the distance – another American import)

State itself built the railway; more often a company, having obtained State approval, would be granted public lands in the area which it was to serve, and these could be sold to pay for the construction. As it turned out, most of these grants became very profitable investments, since the company usually agreed in return to carry government freight at a nominal charge, and as the years went by the value of this service far outweighed the original consideration. These old arrangements were only generally cancelled during the 1950s.

The effect of this encouragement was to accelerate construction greatly. With an enormous area of virgin land ripe for trade and settlement American expansion soon became completely dependent on railways, and in such a vast country it was many years before competitive lines became at all common. As we shall see, the speed with which railways were built had some important technical effects. But it also soon showed up in statistics. By 1835, there were some 1,600 miles of railway in the world; 800 of them were in the United States.

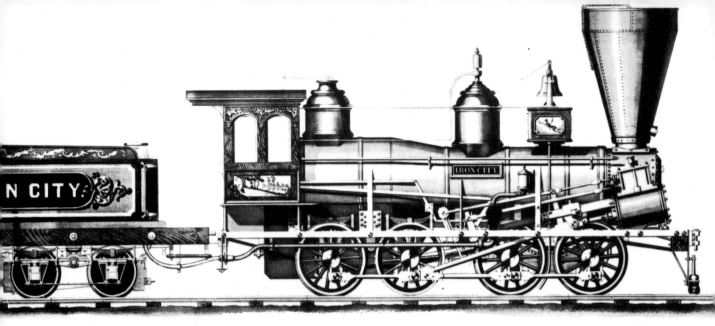

37 This 0-8-0, built by Baldwin of Philadelphia in the 1850s, was one of a series of engines intended for heavy freight service in hilly country; American locomotive design had made giant strides in the fifteen years since the *Lafayette* [figure 54]

In most of Europe matters were arranged quite differently. Generally, the State moved first. The first country to establish a railway system was Belgium, where the main trunk lines were deliberately planned shortly after independence was achieved and built by the government as an act of policy between 1836 and 1844. Once built, they were also worked by the State. Private companies were, however, encouraged to build secondary lines.

In France railway development was at first hindered by argument about the rival merits of the English or Belgian systems of organization. In the event, the Law of June 11th, 1842 established a system of seven trunk lines radiating from Paris, with two transverse connections in the south and east. These were to be built by or on behalf of the government,

38 Share certificate of a westward extension of the Stockton and Darlington during the 1840s

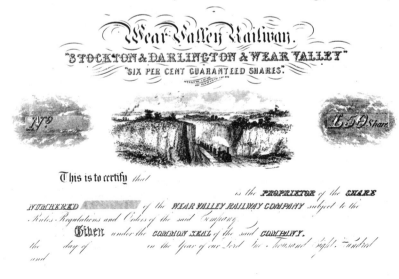

and when completed their working was to be contracted out to private companies, on whatever terms could be arranged by means of competitive tendering. The overall effect was that the French government accepted the responsibility of providing a track for railway, as well as for road-users, and ensured that a railway network was built economically and well, while avoiding wasteful overlapping and competition. On the other hand, the system of tendering for contracts at first encouraged parsimony and exploitation of their monopolies by the companies, and these evils were not wholly remedied until after the re-establishment of the Republic in 1871.

In Germany, which was at this time a patchwork of independent states, railways were generally built and worked by the governments concerned, except at first in Prussia; but even there, where companies were allowed a freer hand, the State controlled the layout of the system absolutely and guaranteed each company from competition. In Russia it was intended that railways should be built and worked by private companies, but although the Czar promised to give freely all the land, timber, and stone needed, and several public-spirited nobles came forward with the offer to lend their serfs without charge (merely stipulating that they should be properly fed), shareholders were reluctant. Finally,

39 A medal struck to commemorate the passing of the Law of 11 June 1842, which established the pattern of the French railway system; the Republic is dispatching winged messengers to two, and trains to four corners of the compass

40 The restored *Adler*, built by Robert Stephenson & Sons, the original locomotive of Germany's first steam railway (the short line from Nuremberg to Furth, opened in 1835), seen on a recent excursion

41 A toylike 2-2-2 running on a very early industrial narrow-gauge line at the beet-sugar factory at Hornu, near Mons, Belgium in the 1850s

42 (*opposite*) A train from Trieste to Vienna on the Sudbahn of Austria-Hungary in the 1850s, crossing the bridge over the old Trieste highway near Ober-Laibach

in 1842, the government was obliged to set an example by constructing the St Petersburg-Moscow main line itself. Italy had by 1850 only a few short isolated railways, and Spain only one. In each case the delay was due mainly to political reasons.

In their various ways, therefore, the countries of Europe and Hudson line when its first locomotive, the infamous *De Witt Clinton*, failed on the opening day in 1831 and the second train had to be hauled by horses. But even more important than pulling power was the ability to stay on the rails, and in this respect the old four-wheelers were deficient. The most famous example of this was the *John Bull*, built by Robert Stephenson in 1831 for the Camden and Amboy Railroad [figure 50].

avoided the extravagances of the British Railway Mania. Opinions in Britain were divided on whether the cure was worse than the disease. During the 1840s many considered that the Continental system was the best and most economical. In later years, when main-line construction had

slowed down and the demoralizing effects of a State subsidy on a private monopoly were becoming obvious, opinion changed and the broadest possible measure of competition was said to be the best way of ensuring an efficient railway system. Today the immense wastefulness of this has been rediscovered, and since we no longer have any political objections to curbing the undesirable activities of monopolies by State regulation (which is much cheaper than competition and, with reasonable goodwill, much more likely to be effective), we now appreciate the advantages of having an economically-planned basic route structure.

All these political matters, whatever their historical interest, may seem remote from the technicalities of railway construction. But in fact they were quite closely relevant. Generally, in Britain, especially before the Mania, and in France, early conditions favoured slow, steady and methodical survey and building of new lines, and there was time as well as money to make them as perfect as possible. Although the railway's freedom from friction made it possible for a small locomotive to draw a heavy train, it also meant that the effects of gradients were far more important than on roads, and it therefore paid to keep the lines level, even at the cost of building great cuttings, embankments, tunnels, and viaducts. The 112-mile London and Birmingham Railway, built by Robert Stephenson between 1834 and 1838, was perhaps the finest example of these first trunk lines. Except for a short and originally cable-worked drop from Camden Town into the Euston terminus, no gradient on this line exceeded 1 in 300 ($\frac{1}{3}$%), and only three curves on the original route, at Berkhamsted, Linslade, and Weedon, carry speed restrictions to this day – to 75 or 80 mph. (The 80 mph limit through Wolverton is due to the diversion of the line fifty years later.) This involved some engineering works like Tring Cutting [figure 43], colossal for their day,

44 Horatio Allen's *South Carolina* of 1831, an early and unsuccessful attempt at getting two engines for the operating cost of one; the symmetrical design had only one cylinder at each end – which was its weakest point

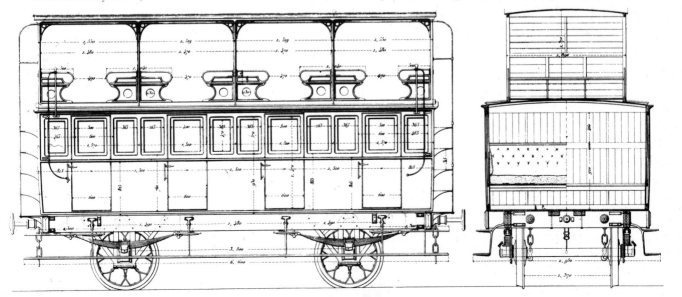

45 A drawing of a double-decked second class 'imperial' coach in use on the Bourbonnais Railway in France in 1857 (coaches of this type, though larger, lingered on in Spain until the early 1960s)

and awe-inspiring even now when one considers that they were built by men with picks, shovels and wheelbarrows. Many of these labourers were Irishmen driven to England by famine. Stephenson knew that he was building for posterity, and the bridges, stations and tunnels were built as if to outlast the Pyramids. Half the line was widened from double to quadruple track during the 1880s, and in every case where the London and North Western varied from the original specification in this work, it was to substitute something less robust. Faint-hearted economists of the '80s and '90s lamented this early perfectionism, but we are still reaping the benefits of Stephenson's foresight. Other similar cases are found elsewhere; France is full of examples, including the Paris–Le Havre line, built by Stephenson's pupil Locke.

The American approach to railway-building was quite different, and it had some indirect effects of great advantage. Here the object was to construct and open the line as quickly as possible; not only was this encouraged by the land-grant system (for property could not be sold until people could reach it), but the roaring economy of an expanding nation insisted on it. Naturally the Americans knew as well as anybody that a line built quickly and cheaply would probably be slow and expensive to work. However, they calculated that once it was built, all the necessary improvements could be paid for out of revenue; and so it proved.

One of the these early land-opening railways was the South Carolina. This was the second in the world to depend entirely on steam power: its first short section opened on Christmas Day, 1830, two months after the Liverpool and Manchester. It chose a gauge of five feet, no doubt because this was a nicely rounded figure, and nobody imagined that it would ever be linked to the standard-gauge of the northern lines. When its 136 miles of track were completed from Charleston to Hamburg, just across the river from Augusta, Georgia, in 1833, it was by a considerable margin the longest railway in the world. Horatio Allen was its engineer, and he had persuaded the company to put its faith in steam by the prophecy, 'In the future there is no reason to expect any material improvement in the breed of horses, while in my judgement the man is not living who knows what the breed of locomotive is to command.'

Yet the South Carolina's first few engines were not very remarkably successful. The *Best Friend of Charleston* [figure 46], which has passed into folklore, was built in New York by the West Point Foundry and was clearly designed by somebody who had studied drawings of Braithwaite and Ericsson's *Novelty*. It weighed only four tons but ran acceptably for six months. Then, on June 17th, 1831 its Negro fireman tied down the safety valve; legend has it that he was irritated by the noise of escaping steam, but more likely he was at the foot of a hill and needed some extra pressure to climb it. However his ascent was made in a different direction. Parts of the locomotive were gathered together afterwards and reassembled; the fireman was not so lucky. The following year Allen, desiring a machine of greater power, placed in service the remarkable *South Carolina*. Mounted on two bogies, with a long symmetrical boiler, central firebox and two chimneys, it was the first prototype of the Fairlie engine, yet since it had only one cylinder at each end it was not a very present help in time of trouble.

Faced with the task of running trains over rough track, up steep gradients, and round sharp curves, the Americans

46 A modern replica of the *Best Friend of Charleston*, built by the West Point Foundry of New York for the South Carolina Railroad in 1830, which inaugurated the service on the first all-steam railway in the New World

47 Two dramatic lithographs of American railway scenes published by Currier and Ives in the late 1850s: (*above*) 'The Lightning Express Trains Leaving the Junction' shows inside- and outside-cylinder variants of the 'American-type' 4-4-0

had swiftly to find ways of improving locomotive performance. First, they started to build engines of greater power, and did so with considerable success. By 1839 the Philadelphia firm of Eastwick and Harrison had produced an engine, the *Gowan and Marx*, a 4-4-0 weighing eleven tons, which on its trials hauled a 423-ton train along the level. In England, the directors of the Birmingham and Gloucester Railway, hearing of the hill-climbing feats of American engines, decided in 1840 to work their new line up the Lickey Bank, a slope of two miles at 1 in 37 (3%), with locomotives imported from Norris of Philadelphia.

But increased power was only one feature of early American locomotive design. It was important, of course; it was poor publicity for a concern like the 15-mile Mohawk

In her original form, this engine was an 0-4-0 of the most advanced type, with outside coupling rods and inside    41 cylinders. Similar engines were giving good service in England, but in her new home the *John Bull* was always leaving the road. There were too many inequalities in the roughly-laid metals, and her springing was not flexible enough to allow her wheels to follow them. After a couple of years, the idea was conceived of adding at the front a frame containing two small wheels, which would act as a pilot and steer the driving wheels round any dog-legged rail-joints or similar causes of possible trouble. The experiment was tried with complete success, even though it meant dispensing with the coupling rods and working the engine as a single-driver, and the 'pilot' became an important feature of design. It was soon redrawn as a four-wheeled 'bogie' and placed under the front end of the boiler. The resulting 4-2-0 [figure 54] was the first distinctively American type, but was rapidly succeeded by an enlarged version with four driving wheels. The 4-4-0, patented by Henry R. Campbell of Philadelphia in 1836, was the standard American all-purpose locomotive for almost half a century.

As we have seen (page 14), the bogie was not really an American invention; Chapman and Hedley had used it under locomotives in pre-Stephenson days. But it soon came to be regarded as one, for in England it found no friends and the Americans adopted it. They quickly realized that a flexible four-wheeled sub-frame offered better road-holding, and also a better ride, for when one wheel dropped into a pothole only half the shock was felt at the bearing. To offset increased weight and cost of bogies, two could be used to support a vehicle of twice the length of the ordinary European four-wheeler. As a result, the standard American

48 The interior of the roundhouse at Nevers on the Paris-Lyons-Mediterranean system, in 1865, with a selection of 0-6-0 and 2-4-0 engines at ease under the domed roof

49 E. L. Henry's painting of the *De Witt Clinton* on the opening day of the Mohawk and Hudson Railroad, 9 August 1831; the use of stage-coach type carriage bodies was very rare and short-lived in America

freight car soon became an eight-wheeler, and while European passenger coach design until very recent times, particularly in Britain, was fundamentally nothing more than a series of stage-coach bodies mounted on one frame, the Americans soon made use of this extra length to alter the layout completely. They introduced coaches which were entered from end-platforms, and a centre corridor with seats on either side; they were cheaper to build, easier to operate, and in many ways much pleasanter to travel in. This technical difference reflected, and perhaps even caused, one of the stock cliché definitions of national character; while Englishmen travelled silently in separate boxes, Americans went about in communities and had to be either friendly or miserable. Ross Winans, of the Baltimore and Ohio, who otherwise gave great benefits to early American railways, attempted to patent the bogie in 1834. He might as well have tried to patent the wheel; the case dragged on for twenty years, ending before the Supreme Court, and he lost at every stage.

Progress in locomotive design was not an American monopoly. Having come closer to perfection so far as the actual tracks were concerned, British and European designers were more concerned to stress economy, speed, and safety as the main desirables for locomotives. Engines soon grew larger and more powerful; having won the prize at Rainhill, the *Rocket* was in a few months found to be too feeble for commercial service on the Liverpool and Manchester, and was sold to an unimportant colliery line near Carlisle. Robert Stephenson led the way, first with the inside-cylinder four-wheeled *Planet* type (of which the *John Bull* was an example), then six-wheelers with sandwich frames and four bearings on each axle (this was a useful precaution with the then rather unreliable forgings, because derailment did not follow automatically from one of the quite common axle fractures). Next he produced his 'long-boiler' design which brought down fuel costs by a more efficient heat transfer in longer tubes. An even more important refinement was the Stephenson patent valve gear (1842), which did away with the complications of the old gab-clutches and handles. For the first time the proportion of the piston's stroke during which live steam was admitted to the cylinder could be varied, with a long 'cut-off' to allow smooth, powerful starts and a short one for fast running, which economised by allowing the steam to expand more fully and therefore do more work. Another eminent locomotive engineer was Thomas Russell

50 The *John Bull*, built by Robert Stephenson & Co for the Camden and Amboy Railroad in 1851, showing the 'pilot' which was added shortly after her arrival in the USA

Crampton, who was one of the first to place cylinders and valve gear outside the wheels, where they were much more accessible for repair. At the time, it was feared that the main limitation on speed was the danger of overbalancing on curves, and it was considered important to keep the centre of gravity as low as possible. This meant, on conventional engines, small boilers or small driving wheels, neither of which were much use for high speeds. Crampton found a way round this difficulty in the late 1840s by placing the driving wheel at the rear of the engine, with the axle behind the firebox. Crampton engines were not very successful in England, but did well abroad; they were fast and very steady runners, and so long as loads were not too heavy, they travelled more quickly than most other types. The French, particularly, loved them, and the SNCF still possesses one in running order, brought out on special occasions [figure 61].

The development of permanent way design is worth noticing. The very phrase 'permanent way' is a survival from a time when engineers wasted much effort in a vain quest for absolute permanence. In building the Liverpool and Manchester, George Stephenson went to great pains with the track, which consisted of wrought-iron fish-bellied rails some fifteen feet long, held in cast-iron chairs on stone sleepers. To ensure perfect line and level these stone blocks had to be very accurately laid on a consolidated foundation, and each one was dropped into place from a height thirty or forty times, while ballast was packed underneath. As this process was impossible on the floating section across

Chat Moss, Stephenson reluctantly laid the rails on wooden cross-sleepers (ties). The disconcerting result was that passengers commented favourably on the much smoother running on this length. The stone blocks were not abandoned for years; as late as 1838 Robert Stephenson was still using them on parts of the London and Birmingham, but the proved superiority of wood was finally admitted, and engineers began to pay attention to chemical methods of preventing decay. On the other hand, the rail of T or I section which had to be carried in chairs, a relic from the days of stone sleepers, was retained for a long time, in Britain until the early 1950s. There were arguments in favour of it: in early days it was unquestionable that for equal weight and cost of metal, this type of rail was stronger because it did not have to provide a broad flat bottom. But when the price of steel fell to that of cast-iron, the balance changed as the flat-bottomed rail did not need chairs.

51 In 'Snowed Up' sectionmen are busy clearing snow from the path of a train marooned in the New England wilds in the depth of winter

In America conditions were different. Timber was cheap and plentiful, and iron was expensive. One or two early lines used stone, generally in the form of foot-square granite blocks of any convenient length laid end to end with an iron strap secured to the upper surfaces, but most used wood, at first in a similar way. This soon had unfortunate consequences. The rolling action of the wheels tended to bend the iron strap rails so that after a while they became sprung. Then the spikes would not hold, and the end of the rail with its sharp point rose high enough for the wheel to run under it, rip it loose, and send the pointed end through the floor of the car. This was called a 'Snake's Head', and the unlucky person sitting over it was likely to be impaled against the roof.

A remedy was sought, and by the early 1840s American permanent way had begun to take on the form which is now the basis of the world-wide standard. Wooden cross-sleepers, or 'ties', supported flat-bottomed rails which were spiked direct to the timber. The vertical weakness of the light rails was countered in American practice by placing the ties closer together, while elsewhere heavier rails were normally used. To this day ties are more closely spaced in the USA, and are still of square cross-section instead of the oblong section used by all other railways.

We have already seen how the South Carolina Railroad came to choose a gauge of five feet quite capriciously in 1830. The question of gauges became a vexed one. Stephenson's 4′8½″ became established in England largely because of a Standing Order of Parliament which insisted on it until 1836, and gained its first footing abroad by the export of

52 A train hauled by two locomotives in the Blisworth Cutting on the London and Birmingham in 1839, shortly after opening

53 A contemporary print of the opening of the railway between Berlin and Potsdam on 22 September 1838

54 The 4-2-0 was the first type of purely American locomotive, a simple, flexible and rugged engine for its day – the *Lafayette*, built for the Baltimore and Ohio by Norris of Philadelphia in 1837

British locomotives and by the desire of foreign engineers at first to play safe by copying everything as closely as possible. But after a while the opinion began to gain ground that the 'coal-cart' gauge was too narrow and restrictive, and here and there broader gauges began to be used. Engineers produced abstruse mathematical calculations proving that such-and-such an additional distance between the rails would be advantageous, perhaps by allowing the boiler water more room to circulate, losing sight of the primary fact that uniformity was itself an advantage. Gauges at one time existed at roughly two-inch intervals from 4' 8" to 6' 6". In Ireland the national standard of 5' 3", which did not exist before, was arrived at by averaging the several different gauges already in use. It was then exported by patriotic Hibernian engineers to Brazil and Australia. The South Carolina's five feet became the standard in the southern third of the United States until after the Civil War; in the northern states, the Erie Railroad from 1841 to 1880 used a gauge of six feet over hundreds of miles, while others were in use elsewhere, and in Canada. Six feet was also used in Holland and by the first railway in Russia, a short line from St Petersburg to Tsarsköe Selo opened in 1837. But the present Russian standard gauge of five feet was imported from America by the two American engineers who built the St Petersburg–Moscow line in 1842, George Whistler, the father of the artist, and Ross Winan's son Thomas. (With them they

47

55 En route from Strasbourg to Paris, a train on the Alsace-Lorraine railways passes through Lutzelbourg in the 1850s; the engine, a 2-2-2 of modified Buddicom type, is creditable – the coaches, apparently less capacious than the luggage van, less so

brought the firm of Eastwick and Harrison, who transferred their locomotive factory to Russia piecemeal.) Possibly a gauge that was different also appealed to traditional Russian xenophobia, since by then 4′ 8½″ was firmly established in most of Western Europe except Spain and Portugal, where the 5′ 6″ gauge took root in the shelter of the Pyrenees.

The broadest gauge of all was adopted in England: Isambard Kingdom Brunel's heroic seven feet on the Great Western Railway. Brunel was an artist and a romantic as well as an engineer, and like Robert Stephenson had sufficient vision to foresee speeds of a hundred miles an hour. But unlike Stephenson he believed that this could only be achieved with a broader gauge. The main line from London to Bristol, although it had two long sections of 1 in 100 gradient (1 %), was laid out and finished as solidly as the London and Birmingham line, but with even greater magnificence, and at first the Great Western's trains were the fastest and most comfortable in the world. By 1848 the Great Western Railway was scheduling average speeds between stops of as much as 57 mph, when average speeds on

56 Barentin Viaduct, between Rouen and Le Havre, in the 1850s, with a Le Havre-Paris train crossing; the engine is one of William Buddicom's 2-2-2s, a design which Buddicom brought with him from England, where it was known as the 'Crewe Type'

the standard gauge seldom exceeded 40. In the same year they ran a special train from Paddington to Didcot, $53\frac{1}{4}$ miles, in $47\frac{1}{2}$ minutes, an average of 67 mph, which remained a world record for over thirty years and was a feat which GWR steam engines of a century later found embarrassingly hard to equal. Brunel's gauge reached at one time from London to Birmingham, Carmarthen, Weymouth and Penzance, filling the area between with a net of branches, yet it was finally destroyed. Technical progress brought up standard-gauge performance to equal it, and it was always more expensive to work because the broader and heavier stock and wider permanent way all cost more. The most difficult problem of all was the trans-shipment of freight at break-of-gauge stations. For the last twenty years of its existence, the broad gauge was confined to the main line from London to Penzance, with a monopoly only west of Exeter, in hilly country where its superiority in speed could not in any case be exercised. It persisted in this area till 1892 only for sentimental reasons.

So far as countries still without railways in the 1840s

57 Berne station in 1860 – many of these simple, dignified and practical overall roofs are still to be found throughout Europe

58 Hanover Junction, Pennsylvania in 1864, with the branch-line train from Gettysburg awaiting the main-line connection (note the American practice of placing the wooden ties close together to counter the vertical weakness of light rails)

were concerned, the pursuit of technical perfection in the British tradition was of less interest than the American demonstration that railways could be built quickly and made to work. Robert Stephenson had told the Swiss that the Alps presented an impassable barrier to railways, and that the only possible method of surmounting them was a vast and uneconomical series of rope-worked inclines. Confronted with this advice local engineers had no option but to book a berth on a transatlantic paddle-steamer and see what the Americans were doing. Such a one was the Austrian, Carl von Ghega, who saw the strategic necessity for a line from Vienna to Trieste, across the mountains, and who therefore travelled to inspect the Baltimore and Ohio in 1842.

By this time the Baltimore and Ohio was forcing its way through the Allegheny mountains whose shadow had first brought it into being. Nothing quite so startling had yet been attempted as was achieved ten years later, when B. H. Latrobe built a temporary zigzag about two miles long with a gradient of 1 in 10 ($10\%$) over the hill through which the

Kingwood tunnel was being cut; a locomotive weighing 28 tons with one coach weighing 15 tons ran safely over this line for six months, achieving a hill-climbing record for ordinary adhesion working that seems likely to stand for all time. But already in 1842 trains had been successfully worked for some years up gradients of 1 in 54 (2%), and that was enough for Ghega. He travelled over the line, inspected it minutely, and having returned to Austria described it in a book. *Die Baltimore & Ohio Eisenbahn über das Alleghany Gebirg*. In an accompanying volume of engineering drawings, he produced evidence in the form of plans of B & O engines, stock, track and structures. For his pains he was called a lunatic, and in 1848 a committee of experts in Vienna, considering the Trieste railway and its crossing of the Semmering Pass, declared that 'it was finally and absolutely senseless to build anything but a cable railway'.

The Alps were admittedly a long way from the Alleghenies, but Ghega was winning despite the scoffs of his detractors. Construction of the rest of the Sudbahn had already started in 1845 under his superintendence, and by 1850 the long and winding 1 in 40 ($2^1/_2$%) climb from Gloggnitz up to the Semmering tunnel was approaching completion, with never a cable in sight. It was time to consider the locomotives, and once again the answer was to hold a contest. This time the conditions were that the engine, with a maximum axle-loading of seven metric tons, should draw a train of 140 tons upgrade at a steady 8 mph.

59 The *Lord of the Isles*, one of Daniel Gooch's *Iron Duke* class eight-foot singles, decorated to haul a train of soldiers returning from the Crimea; built with only minor modifications from 1847 to 1888, these engines were the most famous of all the Great Western's broad-gauge locomotives

The Semmering Trials, held in 1851, must have been spectacular. There were four entrants; the *Bavaria*, by Maffei of Munich; the *Seraing*, by John Cockerill of Seraing, Belgium; the locally-built *Wiener Neustadt*, and John Haswell's *Vindobona*. Noteworthy was the fact that two of the engineers were Englishmen working abroad; Haswell (1812-97) went to Austria in 1837 and worked for the State Railways for the rest of his life. None of the competitors managed to fulfil the conditions. The winner was the *Bavaria*, which achieved a speed of $11^{1}/_{2}$ mph with 123 tons, but this feat fatally overstrained her and having won the prize she was at once scrapped. The *Seraing* came second, achieving 9 mph with the same load, and the others equal last at an inadequate 7 mph.

Yet although the trials were a relative failure, and the railway at first had to be worked by conventional engines, they marked a milestone in locomotive history because they began the development of articulated types. Apart from primitive peculiars like *Puffing Billy* in its eight-wheeled form, and the *South Carolina*, every engine so far had been built on one rigid frame. Even if one end was supported on a bogie, the driving wheels at least were mounted inflexibly. But each one of the Semmering entrants broke this principle. The *Bavaria* was an 0-8-0 with its first two axles mounted on a bogie and coupled to the others by a chain. The *Seraing* was in fact a Fairlie, a direct descendant of the *South Carolina* and of a design supposedly invented, and in any case

60 (*above*) A British 'home' signal (and operator) of the 1850s; post and target turned through 90 degrees to give warning to stop

61 The preserved French Crampton engine, *Le Continent*, built by J. B. Cail in 1852, on one of its recent excursions – though fast, these engines could not manage very heavy trains

62 (*left*) American locomotive decoration in the 1850s and '60s could be flamboyant, as this picture of the *Dakota*, a 4-4-0 built for the Chicago and North-Western by the Hinkley and Williams Company of Boston, shows

patented, some years later by the British engineer-pamphleteer Robert Fairlie. The *Vindobona* was the prototype of the Engerth locomotive, a breed now extinct at any rate in the full-blooded form, in which all the wheels were coupled by rods, with a jackshaft arrangement giving flexibility at the joints. These engines were to be the Sudbahn's standard power for many years. And the *Wiener Neustadt*, although at first it seemed the greatest failure of all, was the ancestor of the Mallet type, which in due season included the largest and most powerful steam locomotives ever built.

Travelling conditions in the early days were spartan. In Europe, passenger accommodation was provided in three or sometimes even four classes. The first-class passenger was seated in comfort (at a price) from the earliest days, and by the late '30s even had the chance here and there of travelling in a rudimentary sleeping car. Second class standards varied, but at the very worst this grade of passenger could be sure of a seat of some kind and a roof over his head. Both these amenities were often denied to the wretched third class, who were carried only on sufferance in trucks hitched to any freight train convenient to the railway company. Slowly conditions were improved, both by the pressure of public opinion and because one or two ugly accidents showed that for reasons of safety alone even third class customers were entitled to better protection. In America there was little at first, and later almost none of this class distinction, and everybody was carried in moderate comfort. When Pullman and

63, 64, 65 and 66 The four Semmering Prize engines of 1851: (*above*) the *Wiener Neustadt* (top), the precursor of the articulateds; the *Bavaria* (bottom), the pyrrhic victor of the contest; (*opposite*) the *Seraing* (top), the forerunner of the Fairlie type, here rather distorted by the artist; and the *Vindobona* (centre), the official Austrian State Railways' standard-bearer

Wagner reintroduced preferential accommodation in the '60s it was on a quite different basis, being provided not by the railway but by a third party. The rail-traveller of the '50s was moved more expeditiously than by stage-coach or canal-boat, but even so, he was 'jammed into a narrow seat with a stiff back in a low-roofed car, whose ventilation in winter was impossible. A stove at each end did little more than generate carbonic oxide. The passenger roasted if he sat nearby, and froze if he sat in the middle. Tallow candles furnished a dim religious light, but the accompanying odour did not savour of religious incense. The dust was suffocating in dry weather, and the begrimed passenger at the end of his journey looked as if he had spent the day in a blacksmith-shop.' Horace Porter, who wrote this account in 1889, may have been an interested party, as he was a Vice-President of the Pullman Car Company, but he was in a position to know.

Safety was another failing at first. Early railways killed fewer of their passengers than the stage-coaches, but while the upset of a coach could clearly be seen as the fault of the driver, either through recklessness or lack of care in inspection, railway accidents when they did occur were much more alarming because they were so impersonal. They were usually caused by broken rails or wheels, or by the error of somebody out of sight, and there was always the suspicion that they could have been avoided by better materials or tighter discipline, and that the real cause might have been meanness, false economy, or in some other way a faceless company showing a greater regard for its shareholders than for its customers. People felt helpless, and therefore angry.

Sadly enough, most lessons in safety had to be learnt the hard way. One cause of loss of life was the habit of locking people into their compartments, for convenience in seat allocation and ticket control, which was at first almost universal in Europe. It ceased in France after 1842, when there was a derailment near Meudon on the Chemin de fer de l'Ouest, followed by a fire. Unable to escape from their carriages, several important notables, including the Admiral Dumont d'Urville, and a large number of ordinary travellers were roasted to death. Yet the custom persisted elsewhere until other similar incidents put an end to it. Fires were common enough in nineteenth-century derailments; if the engine went over first, the wooden carriages piled up on top of it and nothing could stop the whole heap of broken timber, with red-hot coals at the bottom, from going up in flames.

Collisions were the most frequent mishaps. Dr Dionysius

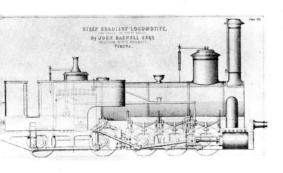

67 (*above*) An Engerth-type locomotive, developed by Haswell after the Semmering trials – all the wheels were coupled together

Lardner, an indefatigable collector of early railway statistics, gave the following figures for accidents in Britain during the 1840s: Collisions $56\%$; broken wheels and axles, $18\%$; broken rails, $14\%$; open switches $5\%$; obstructions $3\%$; cattle on the line $3\%$; and finally boiler explosions, $1\%$. European lines, also mainly double track, had generally fewer trains and were therefore considerably safer, as collisions were reduced proportionately. (Yet the doctor was at pains to point out that the word 'derailment' was not English; it was derived from the French verb *derailler*, and he apologized for the neologism.) At first the prevention of collision was entrusted to policemen who exhibited a danger signal for a certain length of time after a train had passed; the signal was of course no guarantee that the preceding train had not come to a halt just round the next curve. The positive information that it had passed the next station intact, and that the line was therefore definitely clear, could only be conveyed by the electric telegraph, which came into use in one form or another during the 1840s. The information about the state of the line ahead was then conveyed to the driver by various kinds of fixed signal: semaphore arms, flags or balls hoisted up masts, or discs turning alternately broadside on or edgeways were commonest. During the 1850s these fixed signals were sometimes interlocked with points, so that it was no longer possible for a signalman to inform the driver that the line was clear ahead while turning him simultaneously into a siding ending on a high embankment. British and German systems used the same signal to convey both sorts of information, route and interval, often going to great expense and complication, as in the British tradition, to tell him exactly onto which track he was about to be routed. It was only the French who differentiated then (and still do) between the signal which told the driver that the line was clear of preceding trains and the one which told him there was a positive obstruction. By allowing the first type of signal to be passed with caution at danger and forbidding the second ever to be passed unless clear, they removed an ambiguity which is still the cause of accidents elsewhere.

All these signals applied to double lines, general in Europe on main routes from the earliest days. In American practice, where most railways were single track, the problem of preventing head-on collisions was the important one, and before the electric telegraph it was distinctly difficult. The method first used was to run trains strictly by timetable. Extras, when needed, were operated as additional sections of the one time-tabled train at close intervals, and all but the last were distinguished by the engine carrying green or white flags. Any train making an unscheduled stop had instantly to send a flagman out to protect it from a rear collision. Trains were forbidden to run ahead of schedule; but it was when they started to run late that complications began. The places at which trains going in opposite directions were supposed to pass were defined in the timetable, and all freights had to wait there indefinitely for any passenger train however late it was. Trains of equal status waited for each other only 15 minutes; then they set off and ran 15 minutes behind time. Knowing this rule the conductor of a train which was running 30 minutes late could calculate his altered meeting place. Trouble started when both trains were 30 minutes late and ignorant of each other's whereabouts. The resulting chaos was abated only when the electric telegraph was installed and traffic was regulated by a General Dispatcher, issuing instructions to agents at every station, who had the authority to alter and arrange passing places to minimize delays. This method became the standard way of operating single lines in America, and although now superseded on important lines, it is still in very general use, with more or less sophistication, in other parts of the world. Of course, dispatchers were human and could err; many a man made a foolish mistake, realized it too late, and having called out the breakdown gang and summoned doctors, sat helplessly at his telegraph key waiting in agony for the news of the collision.

But whatever their differences, all railways had one thing in common; wherever they began to run, they changed the face of the world. Dr Lardner, visiting America during the mid-forties, wrote, 'Travelling in the backwoods of Mississippi, through native forests where, until a few years ago, human foot never trod; through solitudes the stillness of which was never broken even by the red man, I have been filled with wonder to find myself drawn on a railway by an engine driven by an artisan from Liverpool, and whirled at the rate of twenty miles an hour by the highest refinements of the art of locomotion.' Railways indeed brought civilization to the furthest corners of the world; but they also disturbed some primeval slumbers in the settled farmlands of England. Writing in 1851, John Francis surveyed the wild behaviour of the nomad armies of railway-building navvies, and gave tongue to the ancient lament of the

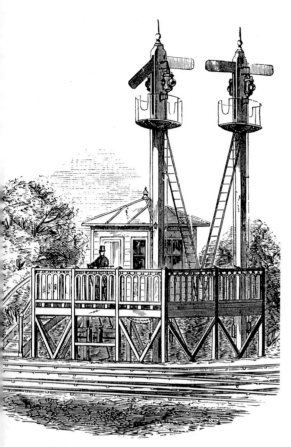

68 Signals controlling a junction in Britain in the 1850s: an early installation where signals and points were interlocked

69 (*opposite*) A group of Camelback locomotives including a 4-6-0 and an 0-8-0 and a train of iron 'jimmy' coal cars at the Baltimore and Ohio shops at Martinsburg, West Virginia, during the Civil War

70 The opening ceremony at Chartres, 5 July 1849; two locomotives stand side by side to receive benediction

71 The disaster at Meudon, near Versailles, on 8 May 1842, which terminated, at least in France, the practice of locking passengers into the train

bourgeois who sees a working man making a lot of money. 'They lived in a state of utter barbarism,' he wrote. 'Some slept in huts constructed of damp turf . . . others formed a room of stones without mortar and took possession of it with their families, often making it a source of profit by lodging as many of their fellow-workmen as they could crowd into it . . . In these huts they lived, with the space overcrowded; with man, woman, and child mixing in promiscuous guilt; with no possible separation of the sexes . . . Drunkenness and dissoluteness of morals prevailed. There were many women, but few wives; loathsome forms of disease were universal. Work often went on without intermission on Sundays as well as on other days.'

Traditionalists thundered thus against these licentious interlopers, who gave simple country folk all sorts of improper ideas. Yet the railways themselves were far more destructive of the old order. For the first time, cheap and swift transport brought travel within reach of ordinary men, and the first lesson they learnt was that their neighbours were men like themselves, with whom they could mingle as friends. This knowlege broke down local loyalties and the last barriers of feudalism, and so destroyed the English aristocracy more effectively, and with less bloodshed, than it had been destroyed in Europe by fire and slaughter fifty years earlier. Railways also made possible the growth of cities, which hitherto could not have been supplied even with the bare necessities of life. It was more than symbolic that the London and Birmingham's Euston terminus occu-

72 The handsome uniforms of the Paris-St
Germain and Versailles Railway Company
in 1840

73 (*right*) A train of the US Military Railroads crossing a bridge south of Washington,
temporarily repaired after destruction in the
Civil War

74 (*below*) A Train Dispatcher, the key figure
of nineteenth-century American-style railway operation

pied the site from which a herd of scabrous and tubercular cows had supplied Londoners with a noxious trickle of tainted milk. When Ruskin thundered, 'Were we not happier when our fields were covered with their golden harvests, than now, when our wheat is brought to us from Dakota?', he was mouthing even greater nonsense than usual.

Thomas Clarke, an American historian writing in 1889, saw it differently. He surveyed the social effects of the first fifty years of railway-building in these words: 'The grand function of the railway is to change the basis of civilization from military to industrial. The talent, the energy, the money, which is expended in maintaining the whole of Europe as an armed camp is here expended in building and maintaining railways, with their army of two millions of men. . . . The moral effect of this on Europe is great, but its physical effect is still greater. American railways have nearly abolished landlordism in Ireland, and they will one day abolish it in England and over the Continent of Europe. So long as Europe was dependent for food upon its own fields, the owner of those fields could fix his own rental. This he can no longer do, owing to the cheapness of transportation from Australia and from the prairies of America. With the wealth of the landlord, his political power will pass away . . . When we consider the effect of all these wonderful changes upon the sum of human happiness, we must admit that the engineer should justly take rank with statesmen and soldiers, and that no greater benefactors to the human race can be named than the Stephensons and their successors.'

# Completing the Networks (1870-1900)

BY 1870, THE RAILWAY SYSTEMS of the more advanced and industrialized countries were mainly complete. In the United States, the first transcontinental line had just been opened, but in the more settled eastern states a fairly dense network already existed. After 1870, new construction in these areas was concentrated on branch lines, filling holes in the map; few new trunk routes were built, and fewer still were needed.

On the other hand, much of the world still lacked railways altogether. Africa was more or less virgin territory, apart from one or two short lines inland from ports like Alexandria or Durban. Asia was in the same condition, except that in India railways had been pushed forward with some vigour after the Mutiny and a nationwide system was beginning to take shape. A start was also being made in Australia and New Zealand. The last thirty years of the nineteenth century saw railway-building on a wider scale then ever before. But they were not quite the same kinds of railway.

The first difference was due to the reopening of the gauge question in the mid-sixties. This time, instead of arguing the advantages of using a width greater than $4' 8\frac{1}{2}''$, engineers were now often in favour of something narrower. The great advantage of a narrow gauge railway was that it was very much cheaper to build. It could turn sharper curves, thus lessening the need for earthworks, which were in any case less expensive because they could be less wide. The trains themselves were also smaller and therefore cheaper. The only remaining question was whether a narrow-gauge line could be made to do a useful amount of work, and until the 1860s this seemed doubtful. A few existed here and there, with locomotives, in factories or mines [figure 41], but this proved little.

The first commercially successful narrow gauge line of any length was the Festiniog, a 13-mile horse-worked two-foot gauge railway in North Wales, which started to use locomotives in 1863. Here conditions were as unfavourable as they could be: the gauge was admitted to be too narrow for long-distance work and the engines had to be undesirably small in order to pass through two tunnels intended for nothing of greater cross-section than a horse. Yet even so steam power paid handsomely, and engineers soon realized

77 Perhaps the most famous railway photograph ever taken: the scene at Promontory Point, Utah, on 10 May 1869, when the Union Pacific and Central Pacific construction trains met, and the first trans-continental line was completed

63

78 A passenger train on the Paris-Orleans Railway leaving behind one of the 2-4-2s introduced in 1876, while two older 0-6-0s stand by in the engine siding – a painting by H. M. le Fleming

that a railway slightly broader, but still much cheaper to build, could deal with any kind of traffic. For long-distance work a width about 50 per cent greater than the Festiniog's would be perfectly adequate; and so lines of three feet, metre, or 3′6″ gauge began to be built. No more broad-gauge colonies appeared anywhere after the mid-sixties; indeed, several were narrowed, and the only subsequent broad-gauge construction was confined to extensions of older lines, in South America, India, Spain, Portugal and southern Australia. Only a few countries, notably China and Persia, chose even 4′8½″ as a standard after 1870; in all the rest of Asia and almost the whole of Africa and Australasia a gauge of one metre or 3′6″ became universal. In America the three-foot gauge was adopted with great enthusiasm, and by

1900 some 16,000 miles of it had been built. The most important narrow-gauge kingdom was in the Colorado Rockies, where it had been established by the Denver and Rio Grande in 1867. At first people were inclined to doubt whether a train running on a yard-wide track could possibly equal the performance and general utility of a normal one, but after a while these fears vanished and a few years later the Superintendent of the D&RG was gratified by this unsolicited testimonial:

Denver, Colorado
20th August 1875

Dear Sir:

It was with some doubts that I applied to you for transportation for my Great World's Exposition, consisting of circus, menagerie, and aquarium, over your line, it having been intimated to me that great difficulty might be experienced in obtaining sufficient accommodations over the *Narrow Gauge*, and even if these were obtained, it would be extremely hazardous, as many of my cases of animals are very high. I have had several years experience in

79 This picture of an impending collision in America in the 1880s was used to advertise insurance — a railway company would have made disaster look less likely

80 The locomotives on the narrow-gauge Denver, South Park and Pacific were fitted with a unique type of spark arrester, which was intended to catch live coals and dump them down a chute on to the track; these two are seen taking water at Golden, Colorado, in 1938, shortly before the line was closed

81 Standard-gauge construction through the Colorado Rockies – a tunnel through naked rock on the Colorado Springs and Cripple Creek District in 1889

transporting my circus, etc., over railroads, and I desire hereby to express to you my appreciation of your arrangements made for us, and to say that never has my World's Exposition been moved more promptly or satisfactorily, your cars being ample to accommodate my stock, wagons, cages, and even the elephant, weighing five tons and standing nine feet eight inches in height... Your cars being so near the ground, renders them much easier to load than those of ordinary gauge. I have met with courteous and businesslike treatment from your employees and agents, and everything was a complete success.

Truly yours,

JOHN ROBINSON JR
Manager, Old John Robinson's Great World's Exposition

The Semmering trials perhaps marked the end of the first stage of building railways through mountain country; but the Semmering was the lowest and easiest of the Alpine passes, and the actual construction of the line had presented no unusual difficulties. It was the narrow gauge that first led the way into really difficult country, and some of the Colorado lines were bold and spectacular. Photographers hauled their enormous plate cameras where mountain goats could hardly follow to record the progress of diamond-stacked engines and wooden cars over chasms and along precipices, through canyons and tunnels in raw rock, across creaking trestles, and in mazes of loop, spiral, switchback and horseshoe curve.

Yet although the narrow gauge led, the standard gauge followed. It, too, could go almost anywhere; it might cost a little more in the first place, but as always there were advantages in spending money at the right time. The main one was that the gauge was *standard*; there was no problem of passengers changing trains nor of trans-shipping freight. The American narrow-gauge boom came to an end in due course. The Denver and Rio Grande itself, having established a main line from Denver to Salt Lake City and a total narrow-gauge monopoly over a large area, found itself menaced by a poverty-stricken standard-gauge intruder, the Colorado Midland. Although it was handicapped by an extremely difficult route, with a hair-raising climb over the mountains and through the Hell Gate pass, the Colorado Midland managed to grab an important share of the traffic simply because it avoided trans-shipment. In self-protection the Rio Grande had finally to convert to standard. The same kind of thing happened elsewhere, but eventually the narrow-gauge found its niche. It could provide a main-line service, and a good one, only in countries where it had an

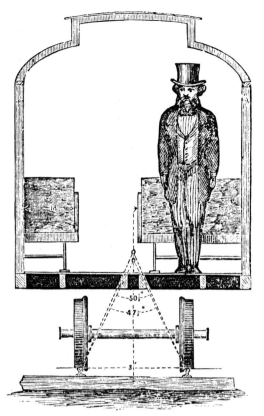

82 A diagram from an American textbook of 1875 proving that three-foot gauge coaches were both adequately commodious, and in no danger of turning over

83 The Georgetown Loop, on the narrow-gauge Colorado Central Railroad some thirty miles west of Denver in the 1880s

absolute monopoly; otherwise it was forced into an inferior position and could only survive as a series of more or less isolated feeder lines, usually in difficult country. Once again, just as with the broad gauge, the practical advantage of uniformity proved to be decisive.

By 1870 engineers had built up an armoury of techniques for driving railways through mountains. The first step was to decide on the steepest gradient to be allowed. By this time 1 in 50 (2%) or 1 in 40 (2½%) was acceptable as an extraordinary maximum, using assisting engines; even more exceptionally, where traffic was less heavy, 1 in 30 (3%) or even 1 in 25 (4%) could be admitted. So long as the average inclination of the valley to be followed did not exceed the figure decided on, there were no major difficulties; any local variations in the level of the valley floor could be smoothed out by building along the mountainside, although this meant rock cuttings, tunnels, and viaducts over side-valleys and was correspondingly expensive. But when the valley became steeper than the railway, construction grew more complicated. It was then necessary to increase the length of the line so that the extra height could be gained without exceeding the limiting gradient, and the local situation determined how this should be done in each case. Sometimes the line could be carried up a side-valley, make a horseshoe curve at the end, and return at a higher level. Often a convenient hill or flat space could be completely circled, with the railway crossing over itself; one spiral of this kind was the Georgetown Loop [figure 83]. In extremity, where no open ground was available, a tunnel could be driven into the mountain, where a train would make a complete circle underground and emerge nearly at the same place, but higher up; these spiral tunnels are quite common in the Alps, and occasional examples are found in other

84 A poster issued by the newly formed New York Central in the early 1870s – their pride in the notable main line in the Hudson Valley, where passenger and freight trains could be operated independently, is understandable, but there were already several 4-track lines in Europe at this time

countries. The most desperate expedient of all was to have a reversing station; when the railway found its way ahead completely barred, the train would reverse and go back the way it had come, again at a higher level. These zig-zags were never used in Europe; they were an American speciality. But examples are still to be found in Burma, India, and most famous of all, in the Andes.

When all else failed, the engineers had to tunnel, and

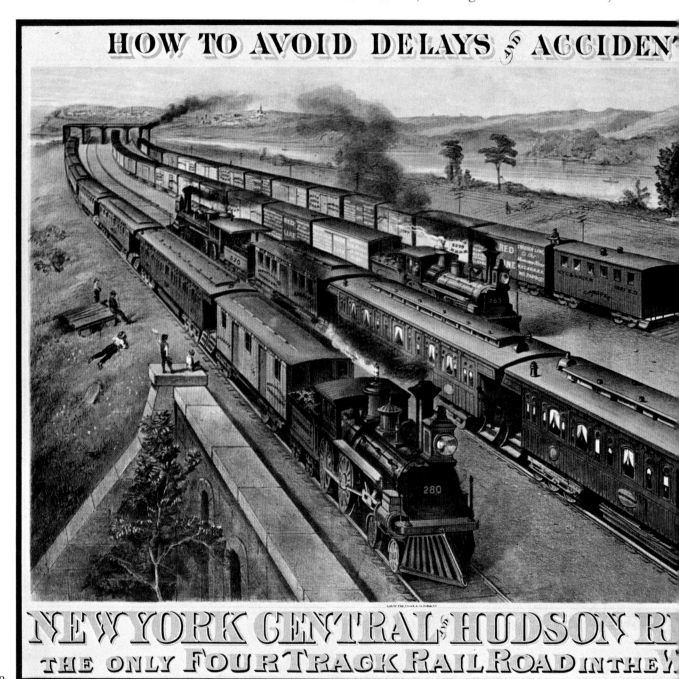

AMERICAN RAILWAY SCENE. AT HORNELLSVILLE, ERIE RAILWAY.

E GREAT TRUNK LINE AND UNITED STATES MAIL ROUTE between New York City and the Western States and Territories, renowned for its Beautiful Scenery, its substantial road bed, DOUBLE TRACKED with steel rail, and its well appointed Passenger trains, equipped with the celebrated Pullman Hotel, Drawing Room and Sleeping Coaches.

85 Another poster of the 1870s, issued by the Erie Railroad, competitors of the New York Central, showing the station yard at Hornellsville, New York, in broad-gauge days

since mountains are always rocky, tunnelling was always expensive. During the nineteenth century, for financial reasons American engineers were even more anxious than Europeans to avoid tunnels of any length, and went to greater extremes to avoid them. Later, following the usual American principle, the railway might be improved and a tunnel built. An interesting example was the crossing of the Cascade Range by the Great Northern Railway, between Spokane and Seattle [figure 88]. When the line was built in 1893, to a ruling gradient of 1 in 45 ($2\frac{1}{4}\%$), it proved impossible to surmount the final crest of Stevens Pass, and a $2\frac{1}{2}$-mile tunnel was necessary. But to avoid waiting until the tunnel was completed (it took seven years to build), a temporary railway 12 miles long was built over the pass, with a gradient of 1 in 25 ($4\%$) and no fewer than eight reversing stations. This was abandoned in 1900 with the opening of the first Cascade Tunnel. But the line was still expensive to work, with many miles of steep climbing and several places exposed to blocking by snow or landslide, and finally it was decided to build a completely new tunnel. This, the second Cascade Tunnel, is $7\frac{3}{4}$ miles long and was opened finally in 1929, shortening the previous route by nine miles.

86 A cartoon published in Britain in 1883, when work on the Channel Tunnel was stopped in deference to the objections of the military establishment

87 Early days on the Brunig Railway: an Interlaken-Lucerne train pauses at a nervous point on the rack-equipped 1 in 11 ($9\frac{1}{2}\%$) climb from Meiringen up to Brunig-Hasliberg

The first really substantial mountain railways were in Europe. The earliest Alpine tunnel was the Franco-Italian Mont Cenis or Fréjus, 8 miles long, from Modane to Bardonnecchia, which took thirteen years to build, from 1857 to 1870. But the first classic transalpine main line was the Gotthard. The Gotthard Railway cuts right across the Swiss Alps from north to south, linking Zurich and Lugano. It was nominally built by a private company, but half the capital was provided by a subsidy from the Swiss, Italian, and German governments. Construction started in 1872 and was completed ten years later, when the $9\frac{1}{4}$-mile Gotthard Tunnel was opened to traffic. The tunnel itself had been a heroic achievement, as ventilation was extremely bad and the rock was both hard and fragile. 177 men lost their lives in accidents, and the engineer, M. Louis Favre, died of a heart attack during a tour of inspection. The approach lines on either side are also spectacular, with several spiral tunnels and a continuous 1 in 40 ($2\frac{1}{2}\%$) gradient, and a great deal of it is built on mountainsides. The other great Alpine routes followed, and the building of each one is a subject for a book.

While on the subject of tunnels, one might well mention a project whose difficulties are not technical, but wholly political, and on which work stopped eighty years ago; the Channel Tunnel. The economic advantages of this have never been seriously questioned, while the technical problems have several times been proved to be unimportant. But the hitherto insuperable objection of the English to having their virginal island's *cordon sanitaire* removed seems to be neatly summed up in figure 86.

Although 1 in 25 ($4\%$) was about the steepest gradient which conventional engines could work reliably, it was by no means the limit, for there was always the possibility of using unconventional ones. These were broadly of two types. Firstly there were some varieties, mainly used on lines serving logging areas and sometimes mines in America and elsewhere, which used reduction gears to drive every wheel, could climb steep grades (up to $10\%$), on rough temporary track, and developed great power at low speeds. Two such locomotives, quite unknown in Europe, are shown in figures 89 and 90.

Secondly, there were engines which in design returned to Blenkinsop and used a rack rail of one kind or another. Racks were expensive and had to be laid accurately, so that they could not be used on temporary lines, but they increased the maximum workable gradient almost to 45°. Most rack

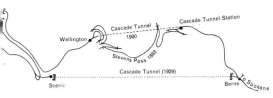

88 The Great Northern Railway's successive crossings of the Cascade Range between Spokane and Seattle

89 and 90 Two types of American geared locomotives: (*top*) the Shay, in which all wheels were driven by a shaft running along one side, and powered by three vertical cylinders mounted beside the boiler, was the most popular; (*bottom*) a smaller type, the Climax, in which the drive was taken by a central shaft

railways were quite short, constructed up mountains so that travellers could ride to the top and enjoy the view. The first of them was in America, up Mount Washington (1867); they exist in many countries, but are most numerous in the Alps. There are two principal systems; the Riggenbach, where two cogged wheels under the locomotive run up a steel ladder laid between the rails, and the Abt, where the steel ladder is replaced by two racks laid close together with the tooth of one opposite the jaw of the other. There are certain cases, notably on the Argentine-Chilean Transandine Railway, where the Abt system was used for main-line work, and long-distance trains, passenger and freight, climb over mountains on gradients as steep as 1 in 10 (10%).

There was another system, invented by the Englishman J. B. Fell, which substituted a smooth centre-rail for the rack, gripped by horizontal driving wheels and special brake-shoes. The main advantage of this, which compensated to some extent for the fact that it was an adhesion system and therefore somewhat affected by the weather, was the greater ease of braking heavy trains on the descent, and so it was used on some fairly important lines. The first was a demonstration railway following Napoleon's road over the Mont Cenis pass, which operated for three years before the tunnel was completed in 1870. The most famous Fell railway was the Rimutaka Incline in New Zealand, where trains were hauled up three miles on a gradient of 1 in 15 (7%) by six Fell locomotives from 1878 until a 5½-mile tunnel under the mountains was completed in 1955 [figure 93].

By the time railways had begun to take mountains in their stride, the demand had grown for them to cover the plains more densely. Trains were the only form of mechanized transport, and communities which were not on a railway suffered great disadvantages by being cut off from their markets by the expense of road haulage. So branch lines had to be built. This raised a financial problem, because although they usually served areas with a much lower traffic potential, they seldom cost proportionately less to build. Unless a company could be persuaded into undertaking them for other than strictly economic reasons, they had to be built by the State, or subsidized. In Europe generally, and further abroad, the initiative came from the government. In France, for instance, branch line construction was formalized under the Freycinet Plan of 1879, which envisaged a standard-gauge railway to every *sous-prefecture*, or in practice every town of any size at all, and a mesh of narrow-gauge lines serving the country

91 One of the last and largest types of 'single-driver' locomotives built in Britain was Johnson's design of 1887 for the Midland Railway: this engine, now preserved, was not taken out of service until the late 1920s

in between. The plan was almost complete in 1914, but construction lapsed after the war and the 13,000 miles of metre-gauge track which once existed in France have nearly all been abandoned. Motor-transport was proving a more economic rural feeder than the railway.

One major motive which private companies had for building uneconomic lines was to protect themselves from competition. British and American railway history during the second half of the nineteenth century often reads like the account of a military campaign; the pace was slower, for a construction team advanced more deliberately than a cavalry charge, but the strategic designs were similar. One often comes across passages like this: 'X, the ambitious chairman of the A & B, resolved to counter the audacious proposal of the C & D to invade his company's territory. Protecting his flank by means of a secret agreement with the neutral E & F, he made a generous bid for the impecunious G & H. The C & D, which had had its own plans for takeover here, struck back, but too late; X was now in possession of a line which struck like an arrow through C and beyond, and now had independent access to the rich traffics of the I & J.' In Britain the warfare seldom really broke beyond the bounds of ordinarily acceptable business sharp practice, once George Hudson and his habit of paying attractive dividends out of capital had been discredited during the aftermath of the Railway Mania. There were of course times when company A blocked the line to company B by leaving trains obstructing junctions, or company C was evicted from its own property or even saw it demolished by company D, but a

92 A rare American nineteenth-century survival, the Mount Washington Cog Railway in New Hampshire – still operating with vintage equipment

93 Two of the original Fell locomotives fighting their way up the Rimutaka Incline, passing the windbreaks on Siberia Curve where once a train was blown off the rails (note the central Fell rail, gripped by horizontal driving wheels and brake shoes)

court injunction could in due course put a stop to these shenanigans and allow the quarrel to proceed in private.

In the United States strong-arm methods were also sometimes used to settle right-of-way disputes. The contest between the Santa Fe and the Rio Grande in 1878 was the most famous case. This concerned the Royal Gorge, an essential pass so narrow that there was room for only one roadbed [figure 94], and whose it was to be was decided by two armies of hired gunslingers. Bloodshed was surprisingly small, considering; the Rio Grande won because their snipers were more effective in stopping the Santa Fe's construction crews, and so their own men reached the gorge first. Admittedly some unpleasantness was avoided by a private arrangement in a back room of a nearby saloon between General Palmer of the Rio Grande, and Bat Masterson, the Santa Fe's commander in the field.

These local uproars were comparatively honest. As always, the biggest villains were elsewhere, behind the scenes. There were fortunes to be made out of railways, and especially in America where legal control was then purely nominal. One favourite method was for a railway to be built by a construction company, which would then go bankrupt, allowing the new line to be purchased much below cost by a favoured few. Another was to promote paper companies threatening to build competing lines; if the victim refused to submit to blackmail and buy its potential rival out, there was no great loss. Most ingenious was for a company, perhaps threatened with bankruptcy, to sell its locomotives, or better still its vital junctions and terminals, to a body formed by its own

94 A train on the Denver and Rio Grande narrow-gauge line through the Royal Gorge, *c.* 1880

95 A rural smithy in the New Zealand back-blocks assembled this monster, apparently out of various spare parts, around the turn of the century for a logging railway at Raurimu

directors; the rest of the railway could then be sold off to appease creditors or to raise money for some other venture, since the new owners could not possibly do anything independently and effective control remained firmly with the original owners. Arthur T. Hadley, professor of Political Science at Yale, wrote sourly in 1889: 'The manager of a large railroad system has in his charge a great deal of property. Two lines of action are open to him. He may make money *for* the investors, and thereby secure the respect of the community; or he may make money *out of* the investors, and thereby get rich enough to defy public opinion. The former course has the advantage of honesty, the latter of rapidity... A Vanderbilt on the New York Central meets a Fisk on the Erie. In spite of his superior power and resources he is virtually beaten in the contest; beaten, because he could not afford to go so close to the door of the State's Prison as his rival.'

America was the home of railway robber barons on the grand scale. But their depredations slowly dwindled. Public opinion was becoming restive, and the law was beginning to make things difficult. Not even Vanderbilt could say, 'The public interest be damned', as he did on a famous occasion, with impunity for ever. But these dinosaurs of pirate capitalism really abandoned railway finance because it was simply not profitable enough in the long run. The average return on American railway investments declined from $2\frac{1}{2}\%$ in 1870 to $1\frac{3}{4}\%$ in 1890, and has never since been very attractive. This may be unfair, for America was built by its railways; but one legacy of these old days is a folk memory of corporate behaviour that was sometimes viciously

96 David Jones' original Highland Railway
'Big Goods' 4-6-0, built in 1894, assisted by a
Caledonian 0-6-0 of 1899 still in revenue
service in 1963

antisocial, which still does the industry great harm after more than sixty years. Another incidental legacy was an extraordinary amount of over-construction. There are now something like 790,000 miles of railway in the world; roughly 220,000 are in the United States, between a third and a quarter of the world total. The richest country in the world can no doubt afford to support them, but there was and is still considerable wasteful overlapping and duplication.

Locomotive design during the last forty years of the nineteenth century developed in three ways; engineers sought greater power, greater speed, and greater economy in running. In the process, the gap between American and European practice narrowed considerably, and ideas were exchanged quite freely over the years; although each country's engines remained quite characteristic, the differences even in appearance became less marked.

97 The Central Pacific's 4-10-0 *El Gobern-*
*ador* was the largest engine in the world
when she was built, in 1883, for service on
the Sierra grades

98 With the disappearance of steam power, several railways are now preserving a few locomotives of great historical interest: a special leaving Haywards Heath behind the Caledonian Railway's solitary 4-2-2, built in 1886 (a notable racer in its day) and a London and South-Western T9 4-4-0 of 1899

99 Snowed up on the Midland Railway's Settle and Carlisle line near Dent in the late 'seventies

Greater power inevitably meant greater size, and size is reflected in wheel arrangements. In the earliest days it was felt that if two sets of driving wheels were coupled together, the locomotive would not be capable of fast running — a reasoning apparently derived by analogy from what happens when you tie somebody's legs together. Hence 'single-driver' locomotives were preferred for fast work, and indeed they were built on occasion right up until the turn of the century. But experience proved that coupled wheels could also run fast, and as loads increased so they became more necessary. Six coupled engines first appeared in the 1820s, as we have seen, and eight-coupled ones in the 1840s. Ten-coupled engines were built in France and one or two other countries in the 1860s but they remained exceptional for some years. Twelve-coupled engines were always exceptional, but were found in several places, including Austria, the United States, and curiously enough Java before 1914. Generally speaking, the principle was to use as few driving wheels as possible for the kind of work the engine was designed to do, to save construction cost. Slowly European engineers came to accept the bogie, and its two-wheeled relative the pony truck, for its flexibility on curves and improved tracking. Their early mistrust of it had some basis; the first types of locomotive bogie had merely a central pivot, like the front axle of a cart — a design easier to explain on historical than practical grounds (it was apt to derail, turn sideways, and act as a toboggan). Once a degree of spring-controlled side-play was allowed, matters improved.

The great variety of possible wheel arrangements has

100, 101 and 102 Three narrow-gauge locomotives offered in the Baldwin Company's
catalogue in 1874 for freight, mixed and
passenger service: the 2-8-0 weighed 26 tons,
and was rated to haul 140 tons up a 2%
grade; the 23-ton 2-6-0 could handle 125
tons, and the 19-ton 4-4-0 75 tons on the
same incline

meant that steam locomotives never became standardized; there were always plenty of exceptions to any rule
that such-and-such a type was best for certain work. Yet a
consensus of opinion was generally found in different places.
In America in the 1870s and '80s there was such an agreement, and three narrow-gauge models from the Baldwin
catalogue of 1874 are shown in figures 100-2; a 4-4-0, a 2-6-0
and a 2-8-0. Some railways preferred the 4-6-0; this was a
handy type as it could be regarded either as an enlarged
4-4-0, an improved 2-6-0, or an economy-sized 2-8-0. For
the last quarter of the nineteenth century these four types
did the bulk of the work in America. There were of course
many other varieties for special purposes; a noteworthy one
was the Forney [figure 103], a tank engine which became
popular for suburban work. Writing in 1889, M. N. Forney
remarked, 'This plan of engine was patented by myself in
1866, and has come into very general use – since the
expiration of the patent.'

So much for greater power. Greater speed, apart from
necessitating proper leading wheels and bogie design, meant
other technical refinements. In the early days it was considered that the secret of fast running was to have driving
wheels as large as possible. Ten-foot wheels were tried, but
this was too much; nine-foot wheels were the largest used
successfully, and these only on Brunel's seven-foot gauge. A
Bristol & Exeter railway 4-2-4 tank with nine foot wheels
exceeded 80 mph in 1854, which was a world record at the
time [figure 106]. But it was found eventually that the better
way to attain high speed was simply to make the wheels go
round faster, and to produce a more free-running engine.
This necessitated improvements in the design of valves.
Until the 1880s almost all engines everywhere had Stephenson valve gear, which is unsuitable for fast running for one
simple technical reason. When the piston reaches the end of
its stroke, its impact has to be cushioned; this is done by
admitting steam into the cylinder for the return stroke
slightly early, and the amount by which this is done is called
the 'lead'. It is a characteristic of the Stephenson gear that as
the 'cut-off' is reduced to allow the engine to work expan-
sively – which is necessary at speed – the 'lead' is increased,
and begins to have a braking effect. Hence engines with
Stephenson gear are normally sluggish when pressed beyond
a certain point. What was needed was a new valve gear which
had all the advantages of Stephenson's while retaining a fixed
amount of 'lead'. A Belgian, Walschaerts, had invented it in

1844 but it was a long while before it gained favour outside Belgium. It reached America, and came to Britain through the New Zealand Railways, which have a curiously long record of technical innovation, and which standardized on the Walschaerts gear as soon as they started to build their own engines in 1889. An executive of the Baldwin works touring New Zealand some ten years later remarked that the NZR had an excellent fleet of engines 'except for that damn silly valvegear'. Back in Philadelphia he tried it out, and saw its advantages. With the simultaneous replacement of the heavy old flat slide valves by lighter piston valves, giving wider port openings, cylinder performance was greatly improved and train speeds began to creep up again.

The third improvement to locomotives was an increase in their efficiency. Basically this meant reducing the pressure of the exhaust steam by getting more work out of it. The first method was by compounding, turning the exhaust from one cylinder into another, where it delivered a second thrust. This had been found satisfactory with marine engines, and the first to try it on a locomotive was a Frenchman, Anatole Mallet, who built a 2-cylinder compound for the Bayonne-Biarritz railway in 1872 [figure 107]. German, English, and American engineers all followed, inventing different systems with two, three, or four cylinders. Eventually three designs won international acceptance: the French de Glehn system, with two high-pressure cylinders between the frames

103 M. N. Forney's patent tank locomotive was popular for suburban and short-distance shuttle work in America; built in 1886, this example survived until recently on the Quincy Railroad in California

104 and 105 New Zealand veterans: (*above*) three 'A' class 4-cylinder de Glehn compound Pacifics of 1906, in their neglected old age fifty years later; (*opposite*) an 'Fa' class 0-6-2T of 1904, which ended her days hauling trainloads of pulpwood to the mills

and two low-pressure cylinders outside; the American Vauclain system, where a high and a low pressure cylinder was mounted on each side, united in the same casting and driving onto a common crosshead; and the German von Borries system, with one high and one low pressure cylinder.

Among the great variety of compound types, quite the most outlandish and almost the least effective was English; the Webb. F. W. Webb was the Chief Mechanical Engineer of the London and North Western Railway, Dictator of Crewe and a prototype Victorian autocrat, who designed an admirable series of conventional engines until he suddenly became smitten with the idea of compounding. His plan was to have two outside high-pressure cylinders and one very large low-pressure inside cylinder; the first two drove one wheel, the third another and, in a misguided attempt to obtain the alleged free-running qualities of 'single-driver' locomotives, the wheels were not coupled. Furthermore, on certain engines, to save the expense of an extra set of reversing gear, the low-pressure cylinder's valve was driven by a plain slip eccentric, which meant that the wheel revolved in whichever direction it had last been turned. Normally this would not matter, as although the engine would back onto its train, it would begin to move forward before any steam reached the low-pressure cylinder and so the slip eccentric would take up its proper position. But if the driver was a little careless or the rails were slightly greasy, the first pair

of wheels would spin, and steam would reach the low-pressure cylinder too soon. The engine would then stand motionless while its driving wheels churned round in opposite directions. This provided endless diversion for the porters and layabouts at Euston, but was no way to commence a successful ascent of Camden Bank. Since this was one of the things that not even his best friends would tell a man like Webb, reams of statistics poured unchallenged from Crewe about the virtues and efficiencies of the Webb system. No other English railwaymen were fooled; after all, they could go to Euston and see for themselves. But several foreign lines fell for it, including the distant Pennsylvania; they ordered, accepted, and paid for one Webb Compound, which sailed from Liverpool gorgeous with bell, headlight, and cowcatcher, and was never seen again. No doubt the Pennsylvania soon enough found out for itself, and drowned the thing in a quiet part of Lake Michigan.

The other fuel-saving development was superheated steam, pioneered in Germany and Belgium. Previously steam had been drawn straight from the boiler, and it was apt to contain a lot of water as spray. This not only wasted fuel (for hot water can do no work) but limited the amount of expansion that could take place before the steam began to condense. Steam on its way to the cylinders was now led through small pipes placed inside the boiler tubes, where it was reheated and dried, and could consequently do much

106 These 4-2-4 tanks, built to J. Pearson's design for the seven-foot gauge Bristol and Exeter Railway in 1853, had driving wheels nine feet in diameter, the largest ever used successfully

107 A train at Bayonne on the Bayonne-Anglet-Biarritz Railway; the double-decked coaches were of a type long popular in Europe. The engine, *Anglet* (built in 1876 by Anatole Mallet), was the first French compound

more work. In fact after some years it was found that with piston valves, Walschaerts gear and super-heating, steam could be made to expand so much in one cylinder that the expense of compounding was hardly worth-while, and after the 1920s compound locomotives were slowly abandoned except in French practice, where they were retained up to the end of steam construction.

Until the turn of the century all these locomotive improvements came from the continent of Europe or from America. Britain rested on her laurels, and no longer led the way. Acworth, writing in 1899, lamented this situation. He first gave an account of recent fast running in France and between Philadelphia and Atlantic City, where the Pennsylvania and the Reading were for the first time in history scheduling trains at an overall average speed of some 65 mph, and he remarked, 'The French maximum legal speeds are lower, the ordinary American maxima certainly not higher, than ours. But the overall speed abroad is higher, because French and American engines are powerful enough to maintain uphill speeds which our engines can only maintain on the level, and on the level, speeds which our engines can only maintain downhill.' He then went on: 'Twenty years ago foreign railwaymen in search of new ideas and improved methods came, as a matter of course, to England. Today the intelligent foreigner thinks there is nothing new in English railway matters to be studied, and he accordingly betakes

108 Two London and North-Western Railway engines exhibited at the Chicago World's Fair in 1894, both Webb compounds: (*top*) a *Greater Britain* class 2-2-2-2 of 1892; (*bottom*) a *Teutonic* class 2-2-2-0

himself to America . . . Today it must be confessed that the tide of progress seems here to have reached high-water mark, if not to be actually receding, while on other shores the flood is still flowing free and full and strong . . . It cannot be that England, which invented railways, whose engineers and contractors and financiers have built railways in almost every country of the globe, will be content permanently to take second rank in railway matters.' But sadly, Acworth's fears were realized.

As engines were able to pull heavier and faster trains, it became increasingly important to fit brakes capable of stopping them. Since loads were heaviest in America, it was not surprising that the Americans led the way. In 1833, Robert Stephenson had patented a steam brake, acting quickly and powerfully on the wheels of the locomotive, but condensation prevented it being used on the train and for the next fifty years carriage and wagon brakes had to be worked by hand. Passenger trains in Europe had brake vans throughout their length, one to every so many vehicles, each manned by a guard; in America every coach had brakes, applied by brakesmen moving from car to car. Similarly American freight trains had brakesmen walking along the roof, whose clubs were useful both for giving extra leverage on the wheel and for belabouring any hoboes who hitched a ride. In Europe men sat in hutches on certain wagons, and in England the system called for trains to stop at the tops of hills

109 An engineer's inspection train in New Zealand *c*. 1885

110 Edwardian elegance – a de Glehn compound 4-6-0, built for the Belgian State Railways in 1905 for express passenger service – a painting by H. M. le Fleming

while a proportion of the wagon brakes were pinned down. If a train failed to stop at the top of the hill, it would assuredly fail to stop at the bottom. Adverse signals also often caused embarrassment. So for reasons of pure self-preservation British goods trains moved with paralytic sloth.

But however they were worked, hand-brakes were too slow to be of any use in an emergency, and engineers turned their attentions to devising a brake which could be applied instantly by the engine-driver to every wheel on the train. The obvious step was to do this directly by compressed air, and an effective straight-air brake began to be used by American passenger trains in 1868. It had the drawback that if the train broke in two the pipe was also broken, and the brake became useless when it was most needed. What was wanted was a system where the brake was applied by air pressure returning to normal; and George Westinghouse produced one in 1875. Each car had a reservoir, holding air at a pressure of 70 (or 100) lbs per square inch, the same as that in the train pipe. When pressure in the pipe fell, the air in the reservoir applied the brakes. After 1887, the Westing-

111 A 2-4-0 of 1890 and a 4-2-2 of 1898 (a short-lived reversion to single wheels), built by the Great Eastern Railways at Stratford – a painting by H. M. le Fleming

house brake began to be fitted generally in the United States and was soon universal on both passenger and freight trains; most other countries followed suit.

But not Britain; or at least, not much of it. Some companies felt that Westinghouse was a rude, pushful Yankee trying to sell them something, and objected. A Mr Smith was working on a British brake which, instead of compressed air, used a vacuum; let him be encouraged instead. And so in 1875 some comparative trials were held at Newark. Unfortunately the result was a little confusing; the Westinghouse train's brakes all came on several seconds quicker than Smith's, but the vacuum train stopped first. Certain companies, whose directors had evidently had that kind of classical education which encourages clear thinking, decided that since the function of a brake was to stop a train, this proved the superiority of the vacuum system; it was only the minority who realized that Smith had merely happened to use proportionately larger brake cylinders, and that the vital test was the speed of application.

For this reason a majority of English railways chose the

vacuum brake and, following their example, so did one or two other countries. Time has proved that this was a bad mistake. As every schoolboy knows, no vacuum can exceed 14·7 lbs per square inch, and therefore any vacuum-powered mechanism is a low-pressure system, inevitably either feeble, sluggish, or both, and always bulky. One very practical drawback of the vacuum brake is that while small leaks in a Westinghouse train-pipe can be heard by a man riding alongside the train on a bicycle, it is an extremely laborious process to find them in a vacuum pipe. For this reason, among others, it has never proved possible to fit continuous brakes universally in Britain, and to this day the majority of British freight trains creep about in the same paralytic manner as in the 1880s. Delays and confusion result, costs rocket upwards, and this one technical error is the most important single reason for the present difficult situation of British railways.

We have seen how the social effects of railways began to operate in Europe before 1870; by 1900 the transformation of man into an urban animal had taken giant strides. Cities could now be fed, and limitations on their growth had vanished. The next problem was that they became so large that people had to be carried daily for miles from their homes to their places of work. Suburban or commuter travel began to be important, and the technical difficulties of running frequent crowded trains had to be faced. The first Underground railways were built, although they did not flourish until electricity was able to replace steam power after 1890. A steam-worked underground railway was a gruesome thing. In America, the Elevated was often preferred, running above the streets on a steel viaduct [figure 115], but it had its drawbacks too: it was noisy and darkened

112 Due to the lack of continuous brakes on British freight trains, they must stop at the head of every steep descending gradient while the wagon brakes are set by hand (here at Llanvihangel, between Hereford and Newport)

113 Wreckage at Norton Fitzwarren on 11 November 1890 after a broad-gauge Plymouth-London boat train, coming down Wellington Bank at 60 mph, had collided head-on with a standard-gauge freight – ten of the fifty passengers were killed

houses. Steam engines were only somewhat less objectionable here; in 1889 an English journalist commented, 'American people are much more patient than we would be under certain sorts of annoyance. Their elevated railways distribute dust and steam in a very impartial manner on the people below, but it is only now and then, when fire and coals are heaped on their heads, dropped into their eyes, or down their backs inside their collars, that they kick.'

Improvements in safety measures continued to be made. Although signalling between 1870 and 1900 adopted few new principles, the old ones were applied much more thoroughly, consistently and universally. The only wholly new invention, with one exception mentioned later, was the electric train staff, a British mechanism which prevented collisions on single line by having an instrument at each end of every section so interlocked that one and only one token, giving authority for a driver to enter that section, could be withdrawn at once. So long as the driver made sure he had the right token, it was foolproof, but it involved placing signalmen at every passing place and was cumbersome and expensive. Few railways outside the British sphere of influence adopted it.

Finally, and not least important, railways began to take more consideration for their passengers' comfort. Roomier, heavier, more comfortable coaches, running smoothly on bogies and heated by steam from the engine, became universal; the old oil lamps were replaced first by gas and then by electricity; sleeping cars became more numerous, and dining cars began to appear, while more and more attention was paid to inside and outside appearance. In most countries, a main-line train in 1900 was a thing of sparkling beauty.

114 Dark satanic mills at Pittsburgh in 1875– railway and river steamers had made possible the growth of industry in what had been virgin wilderness a few years earlier

115 The Bowery at night, showing the New York Elevated at the turn of the century – electricity was already powering the street-cars, and was just about to supplant the Forneys overhead

# The Early Twentieth Century (1900-14)

AS WE HAVE SEEN, steam locomotives were considerably improved during the last few years of the nineteenth century. During the first decade of the twentieth two other big steps forward were taken. The first led to the development of a locomotive type that became a world-wide standard, as characteristic of the first half of the new century as the 4-4-0 had been of the second half of the nineteenth.

Since designers had had such success in increasing mechanical efficiency and maximum speed, the limiting factor now became the rate at which steam could be generated. To increase it, required a larger fire on a larger grate, and this was doubly necessary with the slower-burning, cheaper,

116 and 117 Two independent narrow-gauge railways at Jenbach, near Innsbruck: (*below*) engine no. 2 of the metre-gauge Riggenbach-system Achenseebahn, built at Floridsdorf in 1889, thunders up the rack at an energetic 5 mph; (*left*) a train of the 75 cm-gauge Zillertalbahn pulls out on its way to Mayrhofen, headed by an 0-6-2T, built by Krauss in 1901

118 The world's first class of locomotives designed and built as Pacifics were the New Zealand Railways' 'Q's, thirteen engines delivered by Baldwin's in 1901; here no. 345 is pulling out of Frankton Junction

119 The French experimented with even larger express passenger engines than the Pacifics – here a 4-6-4, or Baltic, built by the Nord in 1911

lignite or anthracite coal that it was desirable to use in many places. The Wootten firebox met these needs, and was first used on a large scale in America; but its wide, deep grate overhung far outside the wheels and it could no longer be tucked away neatly between the frames. It also had to be placed behind the driving wheels, unless these were quite small, and so it generally had to be carried by a rear pony truck. Previously the use of carrying wheels at the back of a locomotive had been rare. In 1895 the Baldwin works built their first 4-4-2 type, basically an enlarged and improved 4-4-0 redesigned with a Wootten firebox and pony truck. This was the first really modern express passenger locomotive. Engines of this wheel arrangement were used to work the flyers between Philadelphia and Atlantic City which had impressed Acworth, and they were christened 'Atlantics'.

But although they were very successful, they were still only improved 4-4-0s, and four-coupled locomotives were becoming obsolete. Once it got moving, the 4-4-2 delivered horsepower in unprecedented amounts, but for starting, the 4-6-0 was still its superior, in spite of its cramped firebox. It was however some years before anybody thought of altering a 4-6-0 in the same way. The first to do it with a series of redesigned new engines were the New Zealand Railways, who in February 1901 ordered thirteen locomotives of the 4-6-2 wheel arrangement from Baldwins. Because of the New Zealand connection, and because they were enlarged Atlantics, it seemed reasonable to call the new type 'Pacifics'.

These pioneer engines, the NZR 'Q' class [figure 118] gave good service for fifty years, but they did not exploit the full potential of the new layout. Neither did the second class of 4-6-2, built the following year for the Missouri Pacific Railroad [figure 121]. It was only when engine builders, still looking for more power, started seriously investigating its

120 A Santa Fe 2-10-2, built by Baldwin in 1912 for heavy freight work in mountain country, in its element on Cajon Pass, California

potentialities, that they discovered the flexibility of the type. There was ample room for the largest possible boiler, as the firebox could be tucked away above the rear truck. Everything fitted naturally into place on a well-organized Pacific; it looked as well-balanced as it was in practice, the first locomotive type to give a characteristic impression of lithe and purposeful power. Other engines had been handsome in other ways; elegant, chunky, thrusting or assertive, perhaps, but never lithe. By 1914 Britain, Russia and India were the only major countries not to have Pacifics in service, except for one or two misunderstood and abortive experiments. Even post-war advances in conventional locomotive design can mostly be looked at as improved Pacifics; versions with eight driving wheels, four wheels instead of two under the firebox, or with other permutations of the main idea.

The other new development after 1900 was the Mallet. We have seen how Anatole Mallet was a pioneer of compounding. Searching for further refinements, while at the same time considering how engines of greater power could be taken round

121 One of the first American Pacifics, built for the Missouri Pacific Railway by the American Locomotive Company in 1902

122 (above) A 4-4-0 built for the New South Wales Government Railways by the Vulcan Foundry, Lancashire, in 1887, and now preserved in working order

sharper curves, he contemplated the old Semmering competitors and conceived the idea of what was in fact two locomotives under one boiler; two sets of driving wheels and cylinders on bogies, one supplying the other with part-used steam. A number of early Mallets were built in Europe, where some still survive, but the type reached its fullest development in America, where in due course it encompassed the largest steam locomotives ever built.

123 and 124 Two Beyer Peacock engines: (left) no. 2 *Villa-longa* (2-6-2T) of the metre-gauge Alcoy-Gandia Railway (in the mountains between Valencia and Alicante), built and equipped by British interests in the 1890s, pauses at the watertank at Desfiladero; (right) no. 5 *Mona* of the three-foot gauge Isle of Man Railway, built in 1874, pauses at Castletown with a winter season train from Douglas to Port Erin

125 Two 2-10-10-2 Mallet locomotives built for the Virginian Railway by the American Locomotive Company for powering heavy freight trains during the First World War

126 One of the Baltimore and Ohio's 1440-horsepower engines built for the world's first main-line electrification, in 1895

127 The Siemens-AEG experimental electric railcar which achieved 135 mph on the Marienfelde-Zossen line near Berlin in 1903

The first American Mallet was built for the Baltimore and Ohio in 1904, and they were taken up at once by other companies. By doubling the number of driving wheels, they effectively doubled the capacity of the typical extremely heavy, not very fast, American freight train at much less than double the cost. The Santa Fe was once a particularly enthusiastic operator of Mallets, having some large-wheeled types for passenger traffic and also experimenting with a flexible boiler (not very happily). Two companies also built Triplex Mallets, with three sets of driving wheels, but this was too much. They failed because the boiler could not supply enough steam, partly because the firebox was cramped by having to allow for relatively large driving wheels underneath it. But by 1918 the Virginian Railway was running 2-10-10-2 Mallets which showed the shape of things to come [figure 125]. In its special field of heavy freight haulage, the Mallet had developed even faster than the Pacific.

Yet although the steam locomotive was still climbing proudly towards its peak development, rivals were already creeping up. Electric power had been very slow to emerge, considering that Robert Davidson had demonstrated a battery-powered engine hauling 6 tons at 4 mph on the Glasgow-Edinburgh main line in 1842. Siemens and others had experimented in Germany and Switzerland in the '70s and '80s, while the New York Elevated (sensitive after all to the shrieks of those with live coals dropped down their collars) had tried out a 125-hp engine capable of drawing an 8-car train at 10 mph in 1885. By 1890 electricity was powering trams, and then underground railways, quite successfully; the world's first main-line electrification was a 3½-mile length through some tunnels on the Baltimore and Ohio [figure 126]. This installation was by the General Electric Co. of Schenectady, using direct current. The other leaders in the field at this time were the firms of Siemens-AEG in Germany, who electrified the short Marienfelde-Zossen line near Berlin in 1901 [figure 127], and achieved a speed of 135 mph in 1903; and Ganz of Budapest, who carried out the first long-distance electrification on the main line from Brigue through the Simplon tunnel into Italy when it opened in 1906. Both European firms used 3-phase alternating current, so the argument between AC (economical current supply, complex motors) and DC (expensive current supply, simple motors) is as old as railway electrification. Ordinary 2-phase AC was a slightly later starter.

Only in the last thirty years have we begun to see how

completely a well-designed electrification scheme will revolutionize railway working. But men of vision were telling us this right from the start. Chicago to New York via Buffalo is 960 miles; steam and diesel trains were or are scheduled to cover the distance in 960 minutes. Yet in 1906 the Chicago and New York Electric Air Line company proposed to build a new, more direct line with trains hauled by electric locomotives making the journey in ten hours overall. The company failed to win support, for commercial reasons (its prospectus claimed that it was actually an advantage that the new line would pass through no cities or large towns *en route*), but technically its proposals even then were perfectly feasible. It has been left to the Japanese to build the first inter-city railway designed from the start for electric traction.

Doctor Rudolph Diesel was already at work, but his name did not yet bulk large. He had built his first successful stationary engine in 1897, but it was very heavy, slow-running, and unhappy when working at anything but a constant speed. These defects caused the failure of the first diesel locomotive, a 1000-hp machine built by the Diesel-Klose-Sulzer Company for the Prussian State Railways in 1912 [figure 129]. The electric transmission which finally countered the diesel motor's relative inflexibility was not yet thought of, and the techniques of the time were not capable of designing a mechanical transmission capable of taking the stress between a spinning thousand-horsepower shaft and a heavy stationary train. It was too much like the old problem of the irresistible force and the immoveable object.

Technical development in other areas continued, and the outline of the modern railway was already visible by 1914. Rolling stock had to be improved to run satisfactorily at the new higher speeds, and wooden passenger coaches were gradually replaced for safety reasons by all-steel coaches. This meant that trains became even heavier, and made further demands on locomotive power. Signalling systems began to move forward again. The idea of remote-controlled electric or electro-pneumatic installations, controlling a large yard or station from one central panel instead of a large number of scattered local signalboxes, which had been pioneered by Westinghouse in America during the 1880s and '90s, began to be adopted elsewhere. Meanwhile the Americans had moved on to automatic signalling on plain line, replacing the block system and its chain of signalmen every few miles; several European countries began to copy

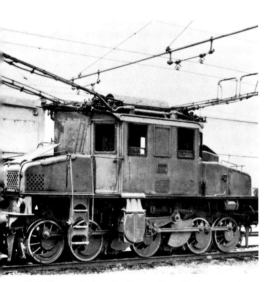

128 One of the 3-phase electric locomotives built by Westinghouse for the Italian State Railways in 1913 – in service at Genoa in 1962

129 The first main-line diesel locomotive, the 1000-horsepower Diesel-Klose-Sulzer of 1912 on the Prussian State Railways

130 The Camaret-Chateaulin mixed of the metre-gauge Reseau Breton near Tal-ar-Groas; this, the westernmost railway in France, is still worked by these 4-6-0 tanks introduced in 1904

it before 1914, notably France. In England, the London and South-Western Railway were creditably progressive in this field, in marked contrast to the conservatism of other British companies. They installed quite a lot of automatic electropneumatic equipment after 1902, and their installation between Brookwood and Basingstoke, twenty miles of 4-track main line including a remote-controlled junction, is still in service, giving results equal to the best obtainable by the latest electronic methods. All these systems still used semaphore arms; the colour-light signal had not yet come.

As we have seen, State ownership of railways was nothing new. In much of Europe the years before 1914 saw the old private companies still strong, even if their privacy was often rather nominal, with their intriguing variety of livery and equipment and sometimes fierce local loyalties. Yet the tide was already turning. Italy provided an interesting example of the gradual trend towards outright national ownership in Europe. Following the unification of the country in 1861, the various lines controlled by the old independent states were taken over and in 1865 their operation was leased out to private companies. The old roughly east-west political boundaries were taken as a guide, and the mainland was therefore divided into three, with the Upper Italian, Roman and Southern Railway Companies responsible for the lines in each section. But they soon found themselves in financial straits, and after the two northernmost companies had gone bankrupt and withdrawn, there was a second reorganization in 1885. This time the boundary was drawn north and south, and there was a Mediterranean and an Adriatic Railway. But the results were no better, the broker's men moved in again, and Italian railways remained a byword for sloth and inefficiency. So in 1905, having tried both ways of slicing up the country, the government nationalized all the main lines. The money could now be found for a big programme of overhauls and improvements, which was finally completed in time for Mussolini to claim the credit. Italian railways have never, except for a few years of suspect book-keeping under Fascism, run at a profit; but it is a species of defective reasoning peculiar to Anglo-Saxons to deduce from this that they should never have been built.

The last years before 1914 have been spoken of as a Golden Age of travel; when the going was good to the furthest corner of the map and all the traveller needed was a ticket. He could plan a journey to Samarkand and foretell his arrival to the minute. Even in the remotest places, once

131 An express for the Simplon line leaving Geneva (Cornavin) in 1906 behind a brand-new 4-6-0

he reached a station, there was a timetable promising a train, and an army of railwaymen standing behind it to guarantee that promise by performance. The railway system was man's greatest technical achievement, and showed the world how common purpose and labour could create something huge and wholly new and good. The traveller from London to Shanghai was whisked across two continents in luxury, but he would see at least something of their peoples' ways of living and could not help realizing how he had come to depend on the care and good will of men whose language and customs differed from his own, but who were also human beings. His train might be snowbound in the Urals or the Carpathians, with wolves baying down at it from the shadow of the trees; but he could be sure that dozens or hundreds of total strangers were labouring with devotion to free him, and meanwhile a well-stocked dining car mitigated his discomforts. It did not matter greatly that the railway itself was at the centre of his vision, for each country's system was a reflection of its customs and habits of mind. Since each employed thousands of men, and was usually the largest single national enterprise, how could this be otherwise?

Nowadays it is fashionable to say that all this came to an end with 1914. Some parts of the world are closed that were open then, but not many. On the other hand, far more people now have money and leisure to travel. For every voyager in foreign parts in 1914, there are now three or four or five. Perhaps only half of them travel by train, and this is a measure of change, but it still gives the lie to those other pundits who dismiss the railway as a spent force. Some colour is lent to this theory by the closure of lines whose traffic is no longer enough to justify men spending their lives in working them. One cannot be happy about railway abandonments: they usually represent a retreat, however tiny or tactical, of the forces of order and service. But the very unimportance of the lines concerned robs them of any but symbolic significance, and in fact despite the growth of competition since 1914, railways now do much more work, very much more efficiently. Their only decline has been in people's awareness of them.

Railways of course have faults. They are often short-sighted, over-conservative, and too easily satisfied with themselves. These are failings of mankind as a whole. Yet they remain a noble achievement, and will be with us as long as civilization exists in anything remotely like its present shape.